Business
Breakthrough

Your Creative Value Blueprint™
to Get Paid What You're Worth

Business
Breakthrough

Your Creative Value Blueprint™
to Get Paid What You're Worth

GAIL DOBY, ASID

Published by Best Seller Publishing®, Pasadena, CA
Best Seller Publishing® is a registered trademark.
Printed in the United States of America.
ISBN: _____

This publication is designed to provide accurate and authoritative information with regard to the subject matter covered. It is sold with the understanding that the publisher is not engaged in rendering legal, accounting, or other professional advice. If legal advice or other expert assistance is required, the services of a competent professional should be sought. The opinions expressed by the authors in this book are not endorsed by Best Seller Publishing® and are the sole responsibility of the author rendering the opinion.

For more information, please write:
Best Seller Publishing®
253 N. San Gabriel Blvd, Unit B
Pasadena, CA 91107
or call 1 (626) 765 9750
Visit us online at: www.BestSellerPublishing.org

Table of Contents

Foreword

By Tom Conley (President and CEO of HIgh Point Market Authority)

I am very pleased to have the opportunity to write the foreword for my friend Gail Doby's new book. Gail graciously agreed to share a copy with High Point Market registrants free of charge which is a generous benefit to our industry.

Gail and her team at Gail Doby Coaching & Consulting have been strong partners with our team at High Point Market Authority and we truly appreciate the part her company plays in education and advancement of the design industry. Improving business skills helps our industry leaders meet their challenges and we appreciate Gail's contribution.

I'm happy to support her book because her mission is to help her clients and all creative entrepreneurs grow their businesses with less stress and more profit.

Gail's new book presents a strong foundation for establishing and growing a successful business. Gail's mission is to help you develop and believe in the vision for yourself, and your firm, and to build the fundamentals for a strong design business.

I encourage everyone who wants to have a bigger, better future to consider this book. Choose to take to heart and put to action the messages in this book and set yourself on the path to success.

Introduction

*The two most important days in a person's life
are the day they are born, and the day they find out why.*

—MARK TWAIN

I'm a creative entrepreneur who has experienced joy and despair with my businesses. I'm just like you—I've celebrated the peaks and endured the valleys. I've felt your pain, and that's one of the reasons why I chose to begin my consulting career with my friend and company co-founder, Erin Weir. I wanted to save you the stress and suffering that I experienced while running a business, which isn't easy to do, even with finance and interior design degrees.

It's true that we teach what we most need to learn, and I learn every day from, and with, my clients. The problems they experience are like puzzles to me—the more challenging the problems they face, the more I want to help solve them. Luckily, solving problems, developing tools, creating shortcuts, and teaching classes are all passions of mine.

A few months ago, I journaled about my goal to write a book. Later that day, I listened to a few videos from teachers I follow, and by the end of the second video, I reached out to my publisher friend and signed up for his services. Within two weeks of starting the writing process for this book, I realized that I have ideas for at least two more books that I want to write. In book two we'll talk about growing your business quickly, and in book three, we'll discuss building your legacy once you've achieved great financial success, so stay tuned.

For now, let's focus on Creative Value Blueprint™, but before we dive in, you may be wondering what a creative entrepreneur is. I define it as someone who earns a living using their unique creative talents. The statistics for most businesses are dismal. Data from the U.S. Bureau of Labor Statistics[1] shows that approximately 20 percent of new businesses fail in their first two years. Forty-five percent fail within the first five years, and 65 percent fail within the first decade. Only 25 percent of new businesses make it fifteen years or more.

Few achieve financial freedom because they lack the business training and skills. They may also have one or more limiting beliefs, such as:

- I'm terrible with numbers.

- I don't understand financials. I won't ever be able to *get* the numbers; they just go right over my head.

- I got into business to express my passion for design, and what I've found is that almost 90 percent of running it is about business. That's not what I signed up for.

- I have to work with difficult people because they are the ones who can afford to pay me.

- I'm overwhelmed. I work and think about work constantly. I have no work/life balance.

- I'm stuck, and I have no idea what to do to get unstuck.

- I'm somewhat successful and want to take my business to the next level, but I don't know what to do to get there.

If one or more of these statements applies to you, I want to encourage you that you can overcome these disempowering beliefs.

---

1. U.S. Bureau of Labor Statistics, 1995–2015

Some of us are naturally resistant to change; we learn and grow through experiencing challenges. I firmly believe that we must encounter obstacles in order to test our theories and our will to succeed. We cannot be truly successful without experiencing some failure and a lot of hard work.

But what if you could work smarter and enjoy yourself more?

How quickly we overcome the pains of our business journey depends on our willingness to learn daily, make mistakes, persevere, solve problems, and get wise counsel and assistance from others who have walked the path before us. That's truly a shortcut in life.

According to research done by U.S. Bank[2] and cited by SCORE (the largest network of volunteer, expert business mentors), the main reasons that small businesses fail are as follows:

- Poor cash flow management skills or poor understanding of cash flow (82 percent)

- Starting out with too little money (79 percent)

- Lack of a well-developed business plan; insufficient research on the business before starting it (78 percent)

- Not pricing properly or a failure to include all necessary items when setting prices (77 percent)

- Being overly optimistic about achievable sales, money required, and what needs to be done to be successful (73 percent)

- Not recognizing or ignoring what the business doesn't do well and not seeking help from those who do see it (70 percent)

As I said earlier, I've had many challenges in my business, some of which I've listed. If you've experienced the following, then this book is for you.

- You are on a revenue roller coaster; you quickly go from being swamped (in a good way with lots of business) and happy to worrying about having enough money to stay in business.

2. Jessie Hagan, U.S. Bank, April 2008

- You aren't earning the income that you want or need.

- You don't have a budget (i.e., a financial model) delivering the results you want.

- You aren't as profitable as you would like or need to be.

- You don't have a marketing plan.

- You don't have a business background.

- You are frustrated with the reality of business versus the passion for being creative.

Seventy-five percent of small businesses are one month away from insolvency! Twenty-five percent of small businesses have two weeks or less of cash in the bank. Seventy-five percent of businesses have a month or less of cash in the bank.

—DAWN FOTOPULOS,
ASSOCIATE PROFESSOR OF BUSINESS, THE KING'S COLLEGE

Before I decided to write this book, I did my research and found the stats to back up what I already knew: it is tough to run a business and even more difficult to keep it going over the long haul. Small business is a big driver of the U.S. gross domestic product (GDP), according to American Express[3]. In fact, 27 million small businesses are responsible for 50 percent of it. However, **60 percent of businesses are not profitable**: 30 percent are at break-even, and 30 percent are losing money. Of those 27 million small businesses, only 1.7 percent of female-owned businesses ever reach $1 million in revenue[4]. For the economy to recover, small businesses must succeed. Ben Franklin once said, "If you fail to plan, you plan to fail." He

---

3. *2018 Small Business Economic Impact Study* conducted by Econsult Solutions, Inc. (ESI) on behalf of American Express

4. *2018 State of Women-Owned Business Report* by American Express

was correct: between the 2008 recession and not having a clear plan, we, too, almost failed. I attribute this to the ridiculous belief that I was smart enough to figure things out as I went. We were running our interior design firm but were not focused on our online business—back then, we thought of it as a side gig. We had zero revenue for the first six months. We also hired a webmaster who turned out to be a complete flake. We didn't have a functioning website until January 2009!

By October 2008, despite these early challenges, we put on a lucrative telesummit with fourteen speakers. We sold $86,000 in classes in thirty days. But our happiness was short-lived—the financial market crashed during the telesummit.

We know how it feels to have the rug pulled out from under us. We nearly failed, but through perseverance and plenty of coaching, we managed to build a strong team and business. When I look at the stats as to why most businesses fail, I know where we made our mistakes. We had a great idea about what we were planning to do but had not written a business plan before starting. Furthermore, there was no one to review it once we had a plan after the business got rolling. At the time, it seemed like it was better to just jump in and get started. (It wasn't.)

We didn't have the financial model figured out either, so there was no contingency plan. What would we do if there was a business downturn? We found out the hard way.

We were also overly optimistic about our achievable sales and the money required to run the business. We didn't have a crystal ball to tell us that 40 percent of designers would go out of business almost immediately after starting.

We were in survival mode for the first few years, and we didn't begin to recover until 2011. During that time, my husband asked me several times to give up and get a job. Being very stubborn and determined, I refused to quit; I knew I could figure out a financial model that was sustainable and rewarding.

In retrospect, our beginner's mistakes were classic and avoidable, and it took me longer than expected to right the ship, but I don't regret the mistakes I made. I take full responsibility for that painful journey because it has given me the grit and determination to succeed and grow. Challenges are what create character and teach us the most impactful lessons.

My goal is to share my counterintuitive ideas and golden nuggets, so you have epiphanies that you can carry with you throughout life. Apply the tips you find here to your business, and you'll immediately see the results.

At the end, be sure to share what you've discovered and applied. I'd love to hear from you!

P.S. I've changed the names of our clients for their privacy.

Your Creative Value Blueprint™

Clients undervalue creative work; they value results. More specifically, clients value tangible results, like furniture in their space. Unfortunately, clients don't understand the true value of the typical creative process required to deliver the end result. That leads to designers struggling to earn what they're worth.

That's why you and every other creative professional need a Creative Value Blueprint™, which is a defined business model that delivers the right balance of creativity, a seamless process, and a profitable financial formula presented in a professional package that clients value and rave about.

Some creatives have a good idea how to produce a beautiful end result, but the bumpy design process leads to distrust and frustration from the client. They may even break their contract and purchase furniture on their own, which leads to the designer losing revenue and profit.

Some creative professionals undervalue themselves and believe that their God-given gift to create amazing designs is so easy that they can't imagine why anyone would pay good money for this natural talent. This requires a belief breakthrough on the part of the designer.

Every element of your business must be dialed in so that you have the confidence to educate and guide your clients to treat you with the respect and compensation you deserve.

CHAPTER 1

Why Your Real Problem Is Often Not What You Originally Thought

A mind that is stretched by a new experience can never go back to its old dimensions.

—OLIVER WENDELL HOLMES, JR.

My mother was a huge influence on my life. She was truly a Renaissance woman—she was a writer, painter, and scientist, among many other things. She believed women should excel at math and science and pushed my sister and me to do just that.

However, her drive for us to achieve didn't always work. When I was in tenth grade, I was in the math club but only lasted one semester. When I was only able to achieve a C grade, I was kicked out.

This affected my belief about my ability with numbers. The real story behind my grade was that I didn't study—I didn't prepare for my tests. I think I secretly wanted to see if I had inherited my mother's genius brain, and I quickly learned the answer was a resounding *no.*

My wish to naturally have the ability to excel was a false and limiting belief that sabotaged my grades. In spite of my failure, I learned my lesson the hard way, but I don't regret it, as learning from challenges has carried me through life. Here's the irony of getting kicked out of math club—I graduated from college with a finance and banking degree. I love analyzing numbers; I just don't love accounting.

Luckily, I don't have to manage the day-to-day numbers. My husband manages our personal finances, and I have an amazing financial team for my business. I just need to understand how to analyze and drive the results, which means I need a clear vision and plan to accomplish my goals.

I use numbers every day to create complex calculations, spreadsheets, and detailed budgets, and I carefully analyze our financial statements. What I learned in college is a very small part of what I've learned over the years through my research and work with clients.

I began offering one-on-one coaching, consulting, and business training in 2010. Since that time, at least half of our clients have cried during their initial VIP Experience™ (our proprietary Creative Value Blueprint™ consulting session), and that includes men. Most of those teary moments happen during our private financial session; sometimes clients are scared that their business finances are a mess and that they'll never be able to make the money they need to achieve their goals.

I often hear our clients say they aren't good with numbers, which typically means they don't know how to read their financial statements (teachable skill), how to budget (teachable skill), how to create or read a cash flow statement (teachable skill), or, most important, how to connect the dots between their personal financial goals (which they may or may not have identified and is easily done) and the financial model that will help them achieve those goals (teachable skill).

A Reality Check

Think about how many times you use numbers every day in your business.

- Requesting or checking pricing
- Marking up goods for resale
- Budgeting for client projects
- Comparing client budgets versus actuals
- Estimating, tracking, and billing time
- Reviewing time billing
- Checking acknowledgments against original quotes
- Creating proposals
- Reviewing bills
- Paying employees
- Paying vendors

You track and manage these numbers all the time, so believing that you're not good with numbers is a false and limiting belief. You *are* good with numbers. You've already proved this.

Let's reframe your thoughts about numbers. You probably aren't a finance major, so don't be so hard on yourself—you may just not know how to understand your financials *yet*. Add the word *yet* to any limiting belief that you repeat about yourself and that will help you remove the label.

You have an incredible ability to learn. You just need to decide to learn the numbers that will make you feel happy, free, financially secure, and rewarded. You are able to learn anything you set your mind to.

You deserve to live an amazing lifestyle and earn money doing what you do best—design. If it is important enough to you, you'll make the decision that having financial knowledge will enrich your life, and you'll courageously seek to understand what has seemed overwhelming in the past.

Think about how much time you spend every day running your business. Out of all the hours you work each day, how many hours do you actually spend on design alone? Maybe an hour? If you work ten hours a day, that's only 10 percent of your time. So, learning how to run your business better is vitally important.

I love helping entrepreneurs make a lot more money by teaching them that numbers are the foundation for the true *art of business*. Yes, you will need to learn some new skills, but if you believe that you can learn them, you'll surprise yourself. When you become courageous and overcome your resistance to learning something new, you'll become confident and assured as the CEO of a business that just happens to provide design or other creative services.

Unfortunately, some people repeat the same message over and over to themselves—that they *just don't get it*. Please ban those thoughts forever, starting today. When these limiting beliefs do creep in, change your thoughts to something empowering. Pre-plan the thought you will use as a substitute, such as: I am learning more and more every day, and I will master my business finances.

When you repeat thoughts over and over, whether negative or positive, you're creating neural pathways, like a groove on a record—so, make sure your thoughts are positive and motivating.

Assess Your Current Reality

Let's take a moment to assess your current reality. Keep in mind that it is a direct result of what you're doing or not doing every day, and if it isn't what you want, then we need to identify what needs attention. It's also important to identify the root causes of these challenge(s), and they may not be what you think.

1. Do you have a business degree?
   Yes | No

2. Do you have a design degree?
   Yes | No

3. Are you a confident decision-maker?
   Yes | No

4. Do you feel calm, confident, and sure of your business skills?
   Yes | No

5. Do you take most weekends off?
   Yes | No

6. Do you sleep well most nights?
   Yes | No

7. Do you take at least two full weeks off per year (no work)?
   Yes | No

8. Do you enjoy your business and work most days?
   Yes | No

9. Do you end your day before 6:00 p.m. most days?
   Yes | No

10. Do you feel your life is balanced most days of the week?
    Yes | No

11. Can someone cover for you if you're sick or on vacation?
    Yes | No

12. Do you set goals for your company?
Yes | No

13. Do you have a written vision for your company?
Yes | No

14. Do you have a defined culture for your company?
Yes | No

15. Do you have clearly defined values for your business?
Yes | No

16. Do you have a marketing plan?
Yes | No

17. Do you market at least ten hours per week?
Yes | No

18. Do you have a business plan?
Yes | No

19. Do you use a contract that has been reviewed by your attorney?
Yes | No

20. Do you have an A-team of employees and/or 1099 contractors?
Yes | No

21. Do all team members have job descriptions (including you)?
Yes | No

22. Do you evaluate employees or team members regularly?
Yes | No

23. Do you know who to hire next and how much to pay them?
Yes | No

24. Do you listen to learn something new every week?
Yes | No

25. Do you read a business book at least once a month?
Yes | No

26. Do you attend regular design or business classes?
Yes | No

27. Do you consider yourself a highly motivated learner?
Yes | No

28. Are you part of a mastermind group?
Yes | No

29. Do you have a supportive peer group to ask questions of?
Yes | No

30. Do you have consultants that help you in your business?
Yes | No

31. Do you currently work with a business coach?
Yes | No

32. Do you have mentors?
Yes | No

33. Do you have accountability partners?
Yes | No

34. Do you have business advisors?
Yes | No

35. Can you solve challenges in less than three days on average?
Yes | No

36. Do you have systems documented in your business?
Yes | No

37. Do you use project management software?
Yes | No

38. Do you have a plan to grow your business?
Yes | No

39. Do you only work with ideal clients?
Yes | No

40. Do you have up-to-date and accurate financials?
Yes | No

41. Do you know how to read your financials?
Yes | No

42. Do you project sales for the year?
Yes | No

43. Do you have a budget and adhere to it?
Yes | No

44. Do you track Key Performance Indicators (financial targets)?
Yes | No

45. Do you feel confident with your pricing strategy?
Yes | No

46. Does your financial team provide dashboards?
Yes | No

47. Does your business make at least 10 percent net profit per year?
Yes | No

48. Are you earning as much as you'd like?
Yes | No

49. Are you making at least $100,000 per year?
Yes | No

50. Are you on track to pay for 25+ years of retirement?
Yes | No

Number of Yes responses _____ multiplied times two equals _____.

Score:

90–100: Congratulations! You're a business rock star!

80–89: You're doing well (though there is room for improvement).

70–79: You're probably feeling a bit stressed (and could increase your skill set).

0–69: Why wait!? Get help to improve your results.

Knowing where you stand is the first step to improving your business. If you didn't score as high as you'd like, don't worry—this assessment gives you clear indicators of what you need to resolve.

Common Entrepreneurial Challenges

Let's take a few minutes to review some of the common issues that entrepreneurs mention when they come to us for help.

- I am stuck and don't know what to do to get unstuck.

- I want to take my business to the next level, but I'm not sure what needs to change.

- I don't have a business degree, and I sometimes feel like an imposter.

- I sometimes take difficult clients because I'm afraid not to take the job, but I wind up miserable. I am stressed and often can't sleep.

- I have no work/life balance. I get home late, need to take care of the kids, and work after they go to bed. I sometimes miss important events and feel terrible when I do.

- My spouse or kids complain that I work all the time, and I constantly get texts and emails in the evenings and on the weekends.

- I don't have a team, and I am burned out from working so hard. There has to be an easier way.

- I get frustrated that my team never works overtime, and I have to pick up the slack to make sure we hit deadlines.

- I'm overwhelmed with the responsibility of running a business. I wonder if I should just get a job.

- I am not earning much money for all of the time I'm working. Surely there's a way to earn more.

- I don't want to run a big company, but I do need and want to earn more money.

- I'm concerned about my financial future. I'm smart, and yet I can't seem to figure out how to do better.

If one or more of these statements applies to you, you know where you're stuck. Congratulations—you've taken the first step! You will solve your challenges. Remember, challenges are feedback versus judgment, and you will always have them—they are part of life. Think of a pilot who sets course from Los Angeles to New York. Along the way, he (or she) will run into weather or turbulence that will require course corrections. Challenges, once they are identified, are data points or opportunities for course correction. Welcome the feedback—it's how you get better.

Creative Value Blueprint™

From the assessment, you've already gotten several ideas about what needs to be fixed, but the reality is that most designers do not have the right business and financial models to achieve their goals. We call this the Creative Value Blueprint™, which is the right combination of all the business elements working together to create the desired financial results.

The Creative Value Blueprint™ is like a flywheel, which is "a heavy revolving wheel in a machine that is used to increase the machine's momentum and thereby provide greater stability or a reserve of available power during interruptions in the delivery of power to the machine."[5] I

---

5. Oxford Dictionary

describe it as the essential knowledge of numbers or what I call the *art of business*. It's understanding the numbers that will drive your results, which will pay for your kid's college, a worry-free retirement, and anything else that life throws at you.

A Creative Value Blueprint™ is the right combination of pricing, profit, cost structure, team, systems, and processes for your business. When the blueprint is designed correctly, it runs smoothly and generates the profit you need to support your lifestyle, dreams, and financial freedom goals.

Building a strong business foundation also requires complete clarity about your vision, values, goals, brand, and team structure. When the Creative Value Blueprint™ has been identified for your business, then you can propel it to new heights with a well-planned marketing strategy. You don't want to overwhelm your current machine with too much marketing until your foundation is rock solid.

Once your flywheel is running smoothly, your business will generate a surplus of money so that you can give back generously to charity, a church, your family, and anything else that you value.

Keep in mind that as your business grows, you'll need to make the appropriate financial adjustments for each new level you're trying to achieve. You'll need a new, customized formula for these different phases.

In this book, my goal is for you to create the basic and essential foundation for your successful business. I will also help you understand some simple financial principles and formulas that I learned along the way, which will give you more clarity about how to achieve the life you really want.

The Principle of Compounding

Dictionary.com describes compounding as "Interest that is added, not only to the principal of a loan or savings account but also to the interest already added to the loan or account; interest paid on interest." Darren Hardy, author and former publisher of *Success* magazine, gives us an example: "You have the choice of taking $1 million right now or a single penny that doubles in value every day for thirty-one days. If you picked the penny, you'd have $10,737,418.24 on day thirty-one. Or if you are a writer who wrote 2,000 words a day, in thirty days, you'd have a novel" (Hardy 2020, *The Compound Effect*, Hachette Go).

Let's now apply Darren's example to your business:

Write down how much you will receive in client payments (your revenue, which is a combination of what you bill for design fees or hourly rates plus product sales) by the end of this calendar year: $_____.

Would you like to know what would happen if your revenue grew between 5 and 25 percent per year? I have created a quick video about compounded growth that will show you exactly where your finances could be in a decade with that amount of growth. It will surprise you that wealth is indeed possible if you implement the right elements in your business. You just have to be ready to overcome your beliefs that you're not good with numbers or that you're missing something.

Beyond that, you now know that you can be charitable and wealthy, and we want both for you. If you and every other business owner could painlessly contribute 10 percent to charitable and worthy causes, would that motivate and inspire you to build wealth? Where would our economy be if we could get all business owners to understand that they can and should focus on building wealth so that they can take care of their families and communities? What if you and all of these hard-working entrepreneurs could generate surplus wealth that could be contributed to worthy causes? Life would indeed be better for the entire planet. You can tell I'm passionate about you being financially successful because of the ripple effect it will have. Every business counts!

Imagine your life as a successful entrepreneur who understands all aspects of running a profitable business. How will you feel when you've overcome your mental roadblocks? How would you rate your willingness to learn what it takes to confidently run your business and increase your financial and business knowledge on a scale of one to ten?

I have a counterintuitive challenge for you; it's called an abundance exercise. Send the link to this book to one or more competitors so they, too, can discover how important it is to charge what they are worth. As you all start charging more, you'll all earn more. The playing field will be leveled. Let's make this business knowledge available to everyone. Abundant thinking accelerates your success and results in more opportunity for you.

Abundant thinking is a choice. Being generous will help you grow your business and financial confidence while improving your bottom line.

Remember the clients I mentioned who cried during the financial sessions of our VIP Experience™? By the end, the lightbulb always went on when we developed their customized Creative Value Blueprint™. When they finally understand what they need to do to achieve their financial goals, it's a special moment for all of us. We love it when the same clients report that they've grown their business two, three, or even ten times beyond where they started.

Summary

- Your beliefs are the first roadblock you must overcome to achieve your dreams.

- Then you must develop a Creative Value Blueprint™ because business success flows from having an executable plan that includes a financial model.

- Focus on filling your knowledge gaps. Once you apply new knowledge, it results in new skills.

- Skills applied continuously create mastery.

- Mastery leads to confidence.

- Confidence is the ultimate reward that comes from taking the right action at the right time, consistently.

CHAPTER 2

Roadblocks

*The person who doesn't make mistakes
is unlikely to make anything.*

—PAUL ARDEN

Did you know that roadblocks and limiting beliefs can be positive turning points and opportunities? I'm going to show you how to embrace them and step courageously into action. I'm also going to share how a lack of structure and poorly conceived plans can make it very difficult to accomplish your dreams—if you haven't mapped out your success strategy, and you don't have a clear picture of how to achieve your dreams, how will you get to your desired destination?

I suggest that discomfort is actually what you're looking for because it's telling you that you need to pivot and shift. The faster you move toward whatever it is that's uncomfortable, the quicker you can move through that discomfort and build your confidence.

Creating Your Vision

In the last chapter, we talked about assessing what needs to be fixed in your business. In this chapter, we're going to talk about the importance of vision. Vision is often limited by judgment, fear, and doubt.

The space between your current results and your vision is called your *gap*. I'd like you to open your mind and think about what you really want to accomplish, assuming that you can accomplish anything you want. Once your vision is clearly defined, then you can develop an executable plan. It works best to start with your vision and reverse engineer it to ensure you're on the right track.

Write your vision out in the present tense. For example: It's _____ (future year—ten years from now) and I am thrilled that I am running a $5 million business. My business has been so successful over the past ten years that my children have been able to go to college without incurring student loans. I have enough money saved that I will have a comfortable retirement. Running a successful business gives me the belief that I can do whatever I want to do and can fund my passions. I love that I get to work, but I don't have to work.

Now, stop reading and take about fifteen minutes to write a compelling vision for yourself. Make your vision as big and exciting as you can, because you can accomplish anything that you have in mind. Start with a ten-year vision, because you want ample time to achieve your loftiest goals. If you think your goals are nearly impossible to do, you're on the right track. Don't worry about how you're going to do it—just decide that you *will* do it.

Now, think about who you need to be to accomplish this goal. What skills and knowledge do you need to have? What support do you need to have?

Visualize yourself having completed all of these goals. Who is with you? Are you sitting on a beach and smelling the salty breeze because now you can afford to live in a beautiful oceanfront property? Make sure that you develop this vision as a complete story that you can imagine yourself in. Then, I want you to review your vision twice a day and journal daily about your goals as if they were a reality.

Then create a plan that goes with this vision and schedule those dates on the calendar. Again, start with your ten-year vision and work backward.

Next, set some intermediate goals that you're going to complete in five years, then three years, and then in one year. As you create your plan, you'll see that the steps in accomplishing this vision are not as scary as you thought. The key is to add tasks to the calendar that will ensure that you accomplish those longer-term goals.

Then, set one to three goals for each ninety-day period that will help you accomplish your ultimate vision. Hold yourself and your team accountable for achieving these goals during each period.

Then break your plan into thirty-day goals, then weekly goals, then daily goals. If you've created the right plan, then you will easily achieve your vision. As Ralph Waldo Emerson said, "Do not go where the path may lead, go instead where there is no path and leave a trail."

I'd like to recommend a YouTube video called the *10 Minute Clarity Routine* by Dr. Benjamin Hardy. In it, he breaks a larger goal down into actual steps that you need to take every day to keep yourself on track. I think you'll find it extremely motivating. At the end of the video, he shares a link to his thirty-day program, which is a life changer. I highly recommend that you complete it along with this book. It will help you shift your mindset.

The Effect of Mindset on Your Business

After twenty years of operating a beautiful retail store, my client Nina was struggling. Her biggest challenge when we met was having a staff of seventeen part-time employees. When I asked her why she had so many part-time employees, she told me most of them had children after they started working for her, and they didn't want to return to full-time work. She cared about them, so she kept them, even though her business was suffering from service gaps. Every time someone went part-time, it took twice as long for a project to be completed.

When we let our emotions rule, it can prevent us from making the necessary moves to survive and thrive. That's what happened to Nina. She was a caring boss, but she put her feelings ahead of her business's needs and that resulted in her earning less than she deserved. Her business was on rocky ground when she came to us.

Think about how your emotions may be preventing you from taking action in your business. Some of these may include:

- Fear
- Overwhelm
- Anxiety
- Anger
- Despair
- Shame
- Doubt
- Guilt
- Comparison
- Blame
- Worry
- All or nothing
- Overgeneralization
- Scarcity
- Indecisiveness
- Judgment

Negative thought patterns can take a toll on your business and your psyche. Once you understand what is holding you back, and what your fears are, you've completed the first step in solving any problem that you have. You'll be more aware of the inner voice that tells you the following:

- I've never done it before.
- I tried before and failed, and I'll probably fail again.

- I don't know how to do it.

- It's too hard.

- It will take too long.

- It will cost too much.

- I don't want to do it if I can't do it perfectly.

- I don't have the experience, time, or resources.

- I feel like an imposter because I am not a trained designer.

- I'm not smart enough.

- Someone else can do it better.

- I am not worthy.

- I am not good enough.

- I will be embarrassed if I fail.

- I don't feel like doing it.

- I don't want to do it.

- I know what they're thinking and they're judging me.

- I was told I'd never be able to do this.

- I'm afraid I'll make the wrong decision.

- I'm sure I'm going to fail.

Turning a Negative into a Positive

As I said earlier, roadblocks are positive turning points and opportunities—you can embrace them and step courageously into action.

Some people lack structure or well-conceived plans. This makes it difficult for them to get anywhere. If you haven't mapped out your success strategy, then you don't have a clear path to achieve your dreams. It's important for you to understand that a lack of structure is one of the biggest roadblocks that you can have.

Repetitive challenges are what I call *brick wall syndrome*. If you can't see beyond the brick wall, and you're repeating the same mistake over and over, you're creating a neural pathway that will lead to failure or, at the very least, achieving less than your potential. It's a frustrating place to be; in essence, you're staring at a brick wall that appears to be insurmountable.

You don't have to suffer or be stuck. If you can't figure something out within three days, you should seek help from someone who can see the situation more clearly, has helped other people out of your situation, and can give you specific advice to remove or get around the brick wall.

In most cases, your challenge is a mental or emotional roadblock. To overcome it, I've told people: "Just imagine that brick wall in front of you. Put your hand on top of it and move it aside to see your vision." Once people do this, it becomes a visual trigger that they can go back to when they feel stuck.

If you believe that you are incapable of doing something, that's your brick wall; take that belief and move it aside. Imagine yourself accomplishing the thing that you didn't think you could do. That's how easy it is to remove the brick wall. It's important to act, even when you don't feel motivated, and *especially* when you don't feel motivated. We often need to do the opposite of what our brain is telling us to do because we don't want to allow our self-sabotaging patterns to win. Right?

Feeling Discomfort Is Part of the Process

When it comes to overcoming obstacles, author and former business executive Seth Godin says, "The best solution to a persistent, apparently non-solvable problem is to make the problem itself obsolete. Go around it. Cease to need it to be solved. Redefine your process or goal so that the problem is no longer permitted to slow you down. An unsolvable roadblock might be better called 'reality'" (https://seths.blog/2019/03/dissolve-it).

An uncomfortable obstacle allows you to pivot, shift, and move toward something positive. It is a guidepost that tells you that whatever seems negative in the moment is just a temporary fear. Once you step toward the solution or into action, you'll find that your mindset will shift, and you'll realize that whatever you were scared of was the temporary discomfort of knowing that you just didn't have the experience.

Erin Weir has worked with me since 2005. One day, I was talking to her about something that I wanted her to do that she had never done before. Within a few minutes, I could see that she was frustrated with me and resistant to the suggestion.

I asked her what the problem was. She said, "Well, I've never done that before, so I'm not comfortable doing it."

"Well, that's exactly why you should be doing it," I replied. "Trust me; I know that you can do it. I have complete confidence in you. If you just try it, you'll find that you'll know how to do it once you get into action."

To this day, she uses this technique on our employees when they resist her recommendations. When they're scared, she'll push them to try. By doing this, she gets them to see that their discomfort is temporary. The idea is to move through the resistance quickly and believe that you'll build your confidence on the other side.

A Positive Mindset

Roadblocks can be a lack of skills or knowledge, and some people feel like they just can't learn. Remember my belief? I'm not great at math. If I had added the word *yet* at the end of that sentence, then I would have given myself permission to try earlier and more persistently. Consider adding the word *yet* onto any statement that makes you think about what it is you lack. I just can't do that … yet.

As with a negative mindset, positive emotions and thoughts can also affect how successful your business is. Some positive emotions include:

- Joy

- Happiness

- Contentment

- Trust

- Optimism

- Courage

- Confidence

Some positive beliefs are as follows:

- I'm resourceful.

- I'm a great problem-solver.

- I'll figure it out.

- I'll find someone to help me figure it out.

- I don't have to know the answer; I just need to know who has the answer.

- I love to learn.

- I love change.

- There's enough business for everyone.

- I can do anything I set my mind to.

- I'm lacking the results I'd like, which means I need feedback on what needs to change.

- I want progress, not perfection.

With our help, Nina was able to shift her mindset. As you might remember, she was uncomfortable with letting people go who were part-time. This resulted in a problem for her because projects were taking twice as long, and her clients weren't happy.

Her employees struggled with keeping projects at the forefront of their minds, so there was inefficiency in processing information that's necessary to move a project forward. She was better off with a handful of full-time employees instead of several part-time employees. When Nina cut some of her underperforming part-time staff, her net profit immediately increased.

She also courageously moved out of her storefront into a less expensive space. She changed her entire business model from mostly retail sales to traditional design services. She rebranded, revamped her business, and moved her office within three months. Since she made these courageous changes, she has increased her revenue by 49 percent and her net profit by 634 percent in just four years!

Summary

- Fear of failure is the belief that temporary pain will be permanent and that the pain of not being perfect means you are a failure. It means that you believe other people's opinions of you are more important than your opinion of yourself.

- Fear of success is the belief that you aren't worthy of financial achievements, or that you'll lose money if you actually get it.

- A lack of confidence is based on faulty beliefs that can be changed by getting into action.

- Money issues revolve around a lack of information and knowledge. Focus on learning. Find the right mentor or coach to learn what you need to learn. It's a shortcut.

- Workarounds are expensive.

- Having the right team is essential. It costs money and stress to do otherwise.

- Projects take twice as long with part-time employees or contractors.

- Hire slowly, fire quickly.

CHAPTER 3

A Successful Business Is Your Real Art

Being good in business is the most fascinating
kind of art. Making money is art.
Working is art and good business is the best art.

—ANDY WARHOL

Maybe you didn't intend to start a business in the beginning. Maybe you were a hobbyist who had a natural talent that your friends recognized and asked you to use on their home. Maybe you couldn't find a job and ended up starting your own business to fulfill your passion. Maybe you wanted to dabble in design while raising kids, or perhaps you always knew you wanted to run your own design business but didn't realize how complex it was.

When people are willing to pay you for the services you provide, we call it *proof of ability*. Just because you're talented doesn't ensure that your ability will lead to business success.

You may be following your passion for design, and you may not have a design degree, and that's okay. Talent trumps a degree. However, in addition to talent, you need to know how to run a great business. I've seen some designers that are better at running a business than designing, but that's typically the exception to the rule.

Entrepreneurs are often unsure of how to successfully run a business; they struggle and hope they'll figure it out along the way. Structure is your friend. It minimizes mistakes.

Putting the Essential Structure in Place with Confidence

Focus on putting the following pieces in place during your first few years in business.

Your Design Philosophy, Aesthetic, and Brand

Spend some time thinking about your design philosophy—which is your stated beliefs about design. This is a source of inspiration (for example, travel and museums) from which to develop your design style. Write your philosophy down. It could be as simple as a few sentences or fill a page, but it should be no longer than that.

Your design philosophy informs the development of your brand, which is more than a logo or graphics. It's everything that you are and everything you do. Some people think your brand is the visual or outward reflection of your preferences, but it goes much deeper. Brand definitely includes all graphical elements, but it also includes your message, what you stand for, what inspires you, and what you uniquely do that other designers do not do. Your brand is the experience you and your company deliver to your clients; you should want a brand experience that is repeatable by others so that your company experience is cohesive and clear.

Your Unique Style

In the early stages of your business, you may or may not have a defined design aesthetic. Focus on defining your primary style or unique look as soon as possible. Many designers who don't have a clear point of view or aesthetic create a different look for each client. This leads to brand inconsistency, which makes it harder for your ideal clients to know that you're the right designer for them. Not having a clear style also means that your business will be inefficient because it takes extra time to do one-off designs. Don't worry. Even when you have a unique look or style, you can still customize each project for your client.

Create an Ideal Client Dossier

Another step in developing a strong business is having an ideal client dossier. (You can fill this out online.) You should know who you want to work with and who you don't, and you should have multiple ideal client dossiers, depending on the business that you want to do. For example, if you want to do only residential work, then you may just have one profile, but if you also want to take on commercial, institutional, or hospitality work, you'll need an ideal client dossier for each of those types of clients. This is an exceptionally important exercise because you want to know what the criteria will be for selecting the right client for your business.

Financial Model

Also, if you don't have a clearly defined financial model, you are navigating in the dark, which leads to guesswork when pricing your products and services. Many clients come to me when they've lost money for a year or more, but after developing a customized financial model, they are earning a healthy profit within months. Having a financial model is more important than creating a business plan that sits on the shelf. It is one of the most important keys to your success.

Financial Knowledge

Some clients struggle to understand how to read their financial statements, which leads to the ineffective "head in the sand" approach to business management. This lack of knowledge can lead to their confusion on how much money in the bank is theirs to spend and can bring about financial disaster. Clients can max out their credit lines and cards and not have enough cash for payroll. I've seen this happen to business owners, in spite of having millions of dollars of sales and hundreds of thousands of dollars in net profit. It's crucial to understand your financials. Running a business without financial knowledge is like flying a plane with a blindfold on.

Attorney-Reviewed Contract

We've even seen some business owners operating without a contract that was written by an attorney who understands the business of design. It may seem to you that you can't afford to have an attorney review or write your contract, but getting sued or not getting paid could make the investment in expert advice seem like a small price to pay to protect your business.

Build a Strong Team Based on Your Values and Culture

If you're a sole proprietor, you probably feel overwhelmed with the stress of doing everything yourself.

Many hands make light work, so build a team you can rely on, because you can't do it all by yourself. Financial freedom comes from building a well-oiled machine. No one is great at all parts of a business.

And even if you have a small team, you may be struggling with the following:

- It seems easier to do it yourself instead of paying someone to do things that you might have to do over.

- Employees require a lot of time and attention—won't it be more work to have employees?

- You may wonder if you can afford to hire someone now and, if you do, whether you can afford to keep them if business falls off.

- You don't know how to find good employees.

- You don't know how to hire the right people.

- You're not sure who to hire first and how much to pay them.

- You want your team to love you so you are ultra-generous and then they take it for granted.

- You don't know how to train people to do what you do so effortlessly.

- Your team doesn't understand that in order to pay them, they need to track their time and be efficient.

Defining your values will help you make easier and better decisions. Your values will help you choose the right team members and manage them.

One way to determine your values is to think about people you admire and list what you admire about them. Once you identify three to five core business values, incorporate them into your Company Culture Statement. When your culture represents your personal and business values, others will sense it and you'll either attract or repel people because of it, which is a good thing.

When your culture is authentically aligned with you personally, you'll feel peace and happiness every day you share space with others who support that culture and your ultimate vision. Hire and fire to your culture because exceptions create stress.

When you are hiring, determine if the candidate is a fit with your business culture. You can't afford to have employees who don't fit with your brand. You must hire and fire to your cultural attributes. For example, teamwork might be one of your culture words; if you have an employee who is a "lone wolf," then they may not be a good long-term fit for your business.

Conversely, recognize your employees for being a great fit with your culture. What gets measured gets improved, so continuously recognize and support your employees as they show and exemplify their fit.

What Can Make You a Stronger Business Leader?

Now, take time to answer these questions, so that you can determine what you need to do to become a business leader with a clear vision.

- What is the first, second, and third skill you need to develop or improve upon?

- What classes do you need to take?

- Do you need to hire a consultant to assist you?

- What is your goal date for mastering those skills?

- What are your core values?

- How would you describe your culture?

- Do all of your employees embody that culture?

- Do you have a defined ideal client dossier?

- What is your design philosophy?

- Does your brand message reflect all of the elements of your business, including your values, culture, and point of view?

- Do your brand visuals reflect your current point of view?

- Does your brand experience delight your clients?

Systems, Policies, Processes, and Procedures

From our experience, few businesses come to us with systems, policies, processes, or procedures in place, which leads to inconsistent results and unhappy clients and team members. Many owners get by for a while, but not without feeling overwhelmed and frustrated with employees that don't know how to deliver their desired brand experience consistently. Writing processes and procedures is not the most fun thing to do, but structure leads to freedom.

Project Management Skills

Most designers don't know how to manage projects efficiently either. Is that you? You may be winging it or flying by the seat of your pants, as many of our VIPs say to us at the beginning of our relationship. There are many software packages like Monday and Asana that you can use to manage projects, and the key is to create templates for typical projects so that you can assign the tasks to team members.

Marketing

Many entrepreneurs experience a roller coaster of revenue, especially in the early years of their business. When they are busy, they aren't marketing. When the pipeline dries up, they begin marketing again, so the swings in cash flow are stressful and dramatic. When you are the busiest is when you need to market the most!

Marketing during the early stages of business is typically through contacts and referrals. Maybe your kids are in the same school as your prospective clients, or maybe you're involved in the same charitable organization. That's a great place to start; however, to build a sustainable and scalable business, a well-conceived marketing plan and budget will be required to take it further.

By now, you're either feeling very confident that you've got it together or realizing that you have some work to do to get your business functioning properly.

Summary

- Creating a successful business requires structure, discipline, and skills.

- Decide which skills you need to develop first.

- Create a plan for your personal development.

- Design your Creative Value Blueprint™ and financial model to support your lifestyle.

- If you don't have the knowledge and skills you need, seek help— it's the ultimate shortcut.

Structure

Earlier in the book, I mentioned the importance of policies, processes, and procedures. It's not the sexiest topic, but when you have repeatable processes, your business runs more smoothly. You'll spend less time training, less time putting out fires, and less time repeating yourself.

As your business grows, you'll need to update your systems to adapt to your growing team. Roles and responsibilities will change and, as complexity infiltrates your already complex business, you'll need to refocus your efforts on refining your internal structure.

The good news? You can hire or outsource the development of systems and processes if you can't bring yourself to do this analytical and precise work.

CHAPTER 4

Systems and Sanity

*It is when your eyes are open to the mechanics
and behind-the-scenes of your craft.*

—RYAN HOLIDAY, THE OBSTACLE IS THE WAY

Our client Beth came to understand what Ryan Holiday calls *the moment*, which every skilled creative has experienced, when she faced a major health obstacle. Beth originally came to me because she was stressed about her financial situation—she and her husband owned their own businesses but were not making as much as they needed to feel financially stable or secure. They also had different values around money, so Beth was stressed about not having the income and financial reserves that provided peace of mind.

During our VIP Days with Beth, we helped her design her Custom Prosperity Formula™ to take her from beyond the median income for designers at that time to having over $100,000 of reserves in less than a year. We instilled the belief that she needed a system to increase her revenue, as well as her income, and increase her fees through the process of working together. We discussed how she needed financial reserves in case of emergencies. She also realized that she needed to build a business that wasn't solely dependent on her to deliver; she needed to develop processes and procedures for it to run in her absence.

Within two years of our working together, Beth became seriously ill, and we didn't know if she would make it. Her story illustrates the reason why systems, processes, and procedures are so vital to business. Organizing and documenting the structure and operations of your company will ensure that your business can operate without you in case of illness, disability, or even death. Thankfully, we have not had clients experience that yet, but it's better to be prepared than not.

Defining and Documenting Effective Systems

I want to define a few words that may not seem exciting now, but you'll understand why I did by the end of the chapter. According to Merriam-Webster:

- Systems are "harmonious arrangements or patterns."

- Policy is a "definite course or method of action selected from among alternatives, and in light of given conditions, to guide and determine present and future decisions."

- Process is a "series of actions or operations conducing to an end."

- Procedure is a "series of steps followed in a regular, definite order."

When you implement systems, you have a business that can run itself. It will be easier to operate, produce consistent results, and ultimately allow your clients to receive a great client experience.

One of the systems you need to have in place is your brand experience, which is more than just beautiful collaterals. It starts with the inside-out thinking and planning we discussed in the last chapter. Your brand experience is the ultimate expression of a well-run, well-conceived, and smooth operation. It is the essence of your personal vision, values, culture, and unique gifts delivered with a system that ensures that the design details are complete, accurate, and delivered on time in a way that is seamless and well coordinated.

When a system is working effectively, your team will be able to deliver on or ahead of schedule and exceed client expectations. A well-crafted brand experience evokes emotion through the receipt of the experience; what we want for your clients is for them to feel heard, understood, valued, appreciated, elevated, and supported.

It's important to think about how you want your clients to feel at all points in their relationship with you. Once you develop and define your brand experience, you'll want feedback from your clients to ensure that how they perceive your brand is aligned with what you think you're delivering. Often, there can be a disconnect between how you think you're doing versus what a client experiences.

For your firm to deliver a great brand experience, the processes and systems must be teachable and duplicatable so that you can let go of control and be assured that your clients are well cared for, whether by you or by a member of your team.

Effective systems also require great communication, both internally and externally. Without great communication, your clients could become tense, frustrated, and anxious and lose trust. Your goal is to anticipate their needs, expectations, and desires before they tell you.

You may believe that systems and processes remove the spontaneity and creativity of the owner, but that is not true. They remove stress, worry, workarounds, costly mistakes, and frustration for both you and your client.

The Hiring Process

Another one of the earliest systems to define and document is the hiring process, which begins with writing a thorough job description. Then you create an ad that is posted online. Some designers have great luck with craigslist, but Indeed, LinkedIn, and even Instagram can be great places to find your next hire.

You need a great set of interview questions and a process, if you have a team. You want your team to interview for attitude as well as skills. A well-designed hiring process is essential, as your potential employee's first touch with your company is very important.

Next, you need an employee manual for your business—something that includes documentation on your policies—so that your employee knows what your company is all about from the beginning and what your vision is for the company. They need information about every aspect of your business at their fingertips, all the way down to what they are required to do while on the job.

Employee Policies, Processes, and Procedures

- **Employee onboarding** Do your employees understand your business and how you operate? Are they prepared and capable of delivering the kind of service that you want to deliver? Do your employees embrace your culture and values?

- **Employee development** Once your employees have been onboarded, what additional training do they need to continue to improve and grow with your company? Do they have a career path so that they can see the opportunity for growth?

- **Mentorship** How do you and your team mentor your employees so that they continue to develop and deliver the level of client experience that you're looking for? What is your process for mentoring and training your team members?

The Client Experience

From the moment a potential client reaches out to your company, your goal is to take them beyond a one-time client to a lifetime relationship. Every phase of their experience should be seamless so that they become long-term clients who happily recommend you.

To create a strong relationship, you need to understand your client and what they value. What are they concerned about? The discovery of their values, priorities, concerns, desires, and aspirations requires that you have a well-thought-out series of questions (i.e., a programming questionnaire) that you ask your clients to better understand them.

The Contact Process

Some designers use a form on their website to get initial information to determine if the project is of interest. I suggest that you go deeper to ensure that you have a great value and culture fit with your prospect.

The Expectation Process

How do you get that client to agree to work with you and pay you what you require for the value you give to them? How do you ensure that they understand your expectations as you understand theirs so that your relationship is symbiotic? This requires well-orchestrated expectation-setting and onboarding of your clients. For example, some designers have financial conversations before they begin designing for their clients. (Be sure to access our Easy Budget Calculator, one of the tools in our Profit & Pricing Shortcuts, so you can have an educated approach to your conversations.)

In these unprecedented times, it's more complicated to develop rapport and relationships when you're not able to meet face to face. How do you connect with people when you're not in the same space? Whether you're doing this in a Zoom call or having an in-person meeting, develop a step-by-step process so that your client knows what to expect and, conversely, what they need to do to be a great client for you.

The Communication Process

As designers, we often get busy and forget that there is a process that should be followed to communicate effectively with our clients. They need to know what you're doing, their responsibilities, what their deadlines are, and where their project stands on a weekly basis. You also need to be very clear about when they're going to receive billing; this sets the expectation about how much they should put aside and how your billing system works.

The Design Process

Since the design process is complex and most clients are not familiar with it, be sure to graphically present its details early in your relationship with them. Better yet, set your timeline for doing their project and pre-set meetings so they know what to expect by when.

The Marketing Plan and Process

You're going to also create a marketing plan and process to build your business; marketing is something you should be thinking about and doing every single day. Having a referral plan is the first part that you should document—you'll want to know how your clients are going to refer business to you, as well as potential marketing partners, such as Realtors, builders, and remodelers.

- When will you ask for referrals?
- How will you ask for referrals?
- How will you reward your clients or referral partners?
- How will you manage the process of connecting with referrals?

The Sales Process

This begins with handling the first call—as you grow your business and bring on a team, you'll want to provide all team members with a series of questions that they will ask of the people who call in or reach out to your company. It is, therefore, important that your team is well trained on how to handle the initial call.

Assuming the initial call is promising, are you the second point of contact? If so, the second call should also be documented with a thorough questionnaire that will help you understand the client's expectations and desires and the scope of the project overall.

The final step that needs documentation is your contract with the client. How do you develop and deliver the contract? How do you get the client engaged and to agree to move forward with you? We recommend setting a meeting with the client to review all aspects of your contract so that they can get their questions answered and you can read their faces during the meeting.

If your prospects aren't a good fit, will you refer them to someone else? Will you stay in touch with them in case things change in the future? I've had prospects who didn't work with me who have referred me to other people who turned into clients, so assume that every relationship is valuable, even if they don't become clients.

The Finance Processes

Many small businesses do not budget on a regular basis. To us, budgeting is one of the most important processes that you can implement within your business. Your budget helps you set goals for yourself. For example, what size of projects do you want to get? How much will your fees be of the overall project size?

Finance processes can also include how you process payments, how you invoice, how you create proposals, how you process purchase orders, how you work with your bookkeeper, and much more.

The Technological Processes

Technology is another area that few people document. This may include software you use to communicate internally with co-workers and externally with clients and vendors.

In addition, you need to think about developing a Customer Relationship Management (CRM) database. What is your process for collecting information about your clients so that you can market to them in the future? How do you secure financial information, like credit cards and payment processing?

If you use software like Keap or Constant Contact, you can send out regular newsletters, and the full newsletter articles can be posted on your blog with a link from the article. You can also set up email sequences for staying in touch with your clients.

The Final Stretch

I believe that where most clients get upset with their designer is in the last 10 percent of the project. You should have a process for delivering that last 10 percent, ensuring your client is exceedingly happy to the point that they're willing to give you a referral.

Because Beth had systems and processes like these in place during her life-threatening illness and because she had financial reserves, she was able to pay her team, keep her company operating, and still pay herself. Her clients waited for her, and she came back to a business that was still operating smoothly.

Summary

- Core systems must be documented so that your team knows how to do their job and you don't have to continuously repeat yourself.

- Policies, processes, and procedures guide your business, even when you're not able to do so yourself.

- Systems ensure that you can deliver a consistent client experience that ensures satisfaction and referrals.

- Systems ensure quality.

- If you want to sell your business in the future, systems and processes make it more attractive to potential buyers.

CHAPTER 5

Teamwork Is the Ultimate Shortcut

*The most dangerous number in business is one.
One stream of income, one employee, one paycheck, one
supplier, one client.*

—DAN KENNEDY

Due to the remote location of one of our clients, its talent pool is limited. However, the firm has to hire junior-level employees with the right attitude and train them to become valuable members of the team.

The owners learned a lot about developing a strong culture from some of our speakers and discovered that they, too, have a passion for developing something equivalent. As a result of their interest and passion for developing their culture, they've built a strong team of employees who embody their non-negotiable values. In fact, their firm has been recognized as a great place to work in their community.

Success Emerges from Having a Great Culture

Culture starts at the top for any organization. Hiring for culture fit and attitude and mentoring the right people is essential. As I mentioned earlier in the book, firing quickly is also essential. As Apple's Dan

Jacob once said, "It's better to have a hole in your team than an asshole in your team."

Many owners dread hiring staff because they think they can do things better and faster themselves, and they worry about loss of control. That's where the documented systems and processes come in—you can deliver a great result repeatedly, and it doesn't have to be done by you. That alone should be motivation to have a team.

A team can be internal clients (i.e., employees), or it can also be external and made up of contractors, vendors, subcontractors, or referral partners. A great team is essential for you to have time and financial freedom.

Phases of Business

There are three main phases in most creative businesses.

- **Phase 1: Business Breakthrough** $0 to $250,000. This would include a part-time or outsourced bookkeeper.

- **Phase 2: Rapid Growth** $250,000 to $1 million in revenue. Typically, you would have up to three employees, including a bookkeeper, plus yourself.

- **Phase 3: Beyond Business** $1 million. Four or more employees.

If you work alone, you can only work more hours to increase your income. If you take a vacation, you give up income as a solo entrepreneur. If you get sick, no one is earning money to pay your bills or operate your business. There is also no one to take care of your clients.

Building your team is one of the most important things you can do to restore balance in your life and grow your company's finances.

Counterintuitive Ideas

Business owners frequently fall victim to counterintuitive ideas, particularly when it comes to making decisions about employees. If you work through these, you'll have employees you can count on and your business will reach higher levels of success. Let's look at a few.

- **You can't afford to hire employees.** If your employee can generate three to five times what you're paying them, you can't afford *not* to have employees.

- **Your employees are there to make your life easier and do tasks that you don't like to do.** The real purpose of hiring employees is to make money.

- **The more you do for your employees (i.e., showering them with benefits or perks), the more they'll reciprocate by being loyal.** Don't expect appreciation for these gifts, as your employees may expect these perks as part of their benefit package. Expect that you won't get brownie points for your generosity—just decide whether it's something you want to give and be okay if you aren't acknowledged for it.

- **If you are nice to your employees and don't correct them, they'll like you better.** Employees need boundaries. They need direction and accountability to ensure that they're really contributing to your business. It's important to have a boundary between being a great boss and being a buddy boss. You don't want to be the buddy boss. You're not there to be their friend. However, it's a great perk if you have employees who consider you a friend, even if you do correct and mentor them.

- **You should hire people before you need help.** You should wait until every member of your team is working beyond forty hours a week, and you should also have a full pipeline before adding additional people. You can always add people in a particular area by hiring contractors, if needed. Ensure that your cash flow and cash reserves justify the extra investment.

- **Hiring interns or junior employees will save you money.** Hire for experience because seasoned employees will take less of your time to train, and they will make money for you more quickly. It can take up to three years to get an inexperienced employee to the point where they're contributing substantially to your bottom line. Be sure to pay your employees at or above the normal pay scale to keep them happy and producing for you.

In my interior design business, I brought on employees after someone suggested that I should hire. I didn't know the industry benchmarks at the time, so I had too many employees for the revenue my company generated. That led to tight cash flow and stress.

I was also a micromanager; I was fearful of expensive mistakes made by my employees. I had no idea how to manage a team—that was not something we were trained to do in school. Some of my employees did make expensive mistakes and, luckily, I learned on my first job with a Fortune 500 company that it was my responsibility to cover the cost of my employees' mistakes. It's part of your responsibility as an employer to train your team and back them up, even when they do make mistakes. If your employees repeat errors, it is ultimately your responsibility—when they are careless, it's on you to correct and retrain them or it's time to let them go.

It's important to learn from your mistakes. Being a micromanager doesn't work. Your employees want to do a great job if you'll let them. However, they do need training and clarity about what the tasks are, what their deadlines are, and what their accountability is. You can learn to be a great boss; it will come when you are more confident in yourself and when you're willing to let others contribute, instead of telling people what to do.

Summary

- Your team is everything; they are your internal clients. If they're happy, they'll make your clients happy. If they're not happy, your clients will know that there is something that's not right in your business.

- Hiring an experienced employee is cheaper and better than hiring someone who is inexperienced.

- Hiring because someone is inexpensive is a false economy.

- Your team members are like children—they need love, nurturing, boundaries, and especially accountability. They also need feedback, and they need it regularly. Don't wait until it's time to give them an evaluation in ninety days—be sure to do it frequently and consistently while they work for you.

- Culture is the DNA of your company. It's how your team bonds, and it supports your ultimate vision and goals. It's a reflection of you as the leader.

- When to hire is when each person on your current team is working more than forty hours a week as full-time employees. You can either hire part-time people or outsource some of these tasks as the first step in growing your company. Your second hire should be another designer, preferably a senior designer. Hiring essentials include a job description, a pay range, an onboarding process, a training plan, and an offer letter.

- You should fire an employee after two warnings or if something bad occurs, such as a breach of integrity.

- You'll never regret firing bad employees, though you may regret waiting so long.

CHAPTER 6

The Difference Between Leadership and Management

*When you become a leader,
success is all about growing others.*

—JACK WELCH

Leadership is not something that most creative entrepreneurs know how to do instinctively since few have business training. However, if you're willing to act with confidence, you can learn how to lead along the way.

Being a good leader means knowing how to guide your team to create your vision and deliver promises to clients. The heart of leadership is excellent communication—we can't read each other's minds. Exceptional leaders understand this and work hard to communicate what isn't readily apparent in a way that is understood by all stakeholders.

What Makes a Great Communicator?

Communication is a learned skill that can be improved by following a simple process.

- **Start with *why*.** *Why* will get the attention of the majority of people. For example, my second-in-command, Erin, is a *why* person. She can't engage with a task until she understands why it needs to be done.

- **_What_ is the next step of communication.** Spell out the specifics of your desired outcome. I'm a _what_ person. That's fairly common for business owners who are results oriented.

- **_How_ people need to understand the details to accomplish the tasks at hand.** They are _finishers_ who get things done. Erin is also a _how_ person; when we first started working together in 2005, she took my vision and made it come to life. She is also a finisher, and I am a _starter_. Business owners need finishers and _how_ people to take care of the details and complete things on behalf of the owner(s). Keep in mind that _how_ people may sometimes fail to see the forest for the trees; you'll need to keep directing and encouraging them to stay out of the weeds so that they can quickly complete the critical tasks at hand. You will also need to help your _how_ people prioritize what needs to be done if you continue to add projects to their list. They can get overwhelmed because they're used to completing tasks, so be aware that you must limit the number of new projects you start or you'll lose that person due to frustration and burnout.

- **_What if_ people are the brakes of your business.** They ask you to remove the rose-colored glasses and consider what will happen if things don't go as planned. You need _what if_ people on your team, especially if you're an optimistic entrepreneur, which most of us are. Business owners can't do everything; we need someone who thinks about the potential roadblocks so that we can address the issues before they arise. Our chief technical officer is a _what if_ person who keeps us from jumping off cliffs with his measured approach to projects.

Don't Be Afraid to Be Firm

Great leadership means you must be willing to have the tough conversations, put on your adult pants, and face problems head-on with finesse.

I initially struggled with being a leader in my own interior design business; I disliked conflict and was a people pleaser. I still don't like conflict, and I'm still a people pleaser occasionally, but I've learned that employees can be like kids: They need boundaries and clear expectations.

We're all human—we want to be liked, acknowledged, and appreciated. It's our job to coach and mentor our employees or team members to do their best work while saying what needs to be said with tact and positive intent to help people be their best.

I lacked confidence in my leadership skills when I first started my design business. I'd never managed a team. I learned that these feelings are quite common, so know that you're not alone if you also struggle with confidence.

I eventually discovered that I'm not so much a manager but a director, and this is why Erin manages our team. She continually thinks about how others process information and how to train them. If you're like me, you need someone like that as your second-in-command. Your employees must be held accountable for their actions—that requires someone to set the rules and ensure that they're followed to keep the team and company on track, on deadline, and on budget.

You can care about your team while not crossing the line to friendship. It's not much different than having clients become friends during a project; in both instances, we tend to have a difficult time saying no or charging for our time if we cross the friendship line because we want to *maintain relationships*. Be prepared for disappointment if you cross the line and choose friendship over being a leader.

Finally, you are ultimately responsible for all results in your company. Before blaming someone else for a result or problem, take responsibility for your mistakes as a leader. As my husband says when things go off the rails, "Fix the problem, not the blame." That phrase has served me well for years.

Management Versus Leadership

A manager is responsible for achieving an outcome set out by their visionary leader. The manager must ensure that goals are achieved on time and under budget. They oversee the resources and team members to get things done. They must have project management skills, as well as motivational, measurement, and people skills.

A leader sets the vision and inspires people to be on the bus as it heads toward its destination. They provide advice and mentoring to solve problems, but they aren't directly involved with measuring the results throughout the process.

You need both management and leadership within a company. Most small companies are led by a courageous entrepreneur who may be better suited to manage or lead, but not both. However, in the early stages, entrepreneurs have to do both roles. If you're not good at one of these roles, then you should put someone else in charge of the area where you are lacking.

Delegation Versus Abdication

Delegating is one of the hardest skills for new managers to learn. I *love* to delegate. I have learned that if I don't like to do something, or I don't know how to do something, or I simply shouldn't do something because higher-level tasks are a better fit with my level of responsibility or genius, then those tasks should be someone else's responsibility. If you can pay someone less than what you pay yourself to do the same task and they love doing it, hurry up and get delegating.

To delegate effectively, you must decide which position within your firm should be the one to produce a certain result and then create a checklist or processes and procedures to train another person to take over the responsibility. Or, once you assign the task, have your delegate document the steps. After training, have your employees give you feedback on what they've learned so that you can be sure they retained your teachings. Encourage them to ask questions for clarification.

When team members start working on a project, create check-in times to make sure they're on track and follow up with them to be certain that they complete the task on time to your standards.

Abdication is the opposite of delegation. It's the handing off of a task without developing a process to assist with the transition of the role. If you abdicate, you are sure to get poor results. Again, as a business owner or manager, if someone in your company doesn't accomplish a task correctly or on time, ask yourself what you contributed to the situation. You may realize that:

- Your employee heard the message just once—it can take up to seven times before someone truly hears and processes a message.

- Your employee misunderstood what you said but was afraid to ask for the instruction to be repeated. They may feel stupid if they don't get it right the first time.

- The team member interpreted what you said differently from your intent.

- They didn't write down the details in a checklist or have a complete and logical step-by-step process to follow.

- The employee did not ask for clarification.

- They didn't give feedback to ensure what you said was understood correctly.

- They heard the instruction, but it wasn't delivered in their learning style, which could easily result in the message being heard but not understood.

If you must correct an employee, one of my favorite phrases when seeking alignment if things go off track is to say "Help me understand…" When you use this phrase followed by a statement of what you're seeking, you're assuming positive intent by making sure you understand the other person's thought process before making a decision or correction.

Communicating in a Language Employees Understand

Many managers become frustrated when they've told their employees to do something a certain way many times. What they don't realize is that designers are visual people—if you give them oral instructions, they'll remember them 10 percent of the time. You must repeat the same verbal message seven to ten times for it to sink in.

Created in the 1970s, neurolinguistic programming (NLP) is "a pseudoscientific approach to communication, personal development, and psychotherapy," according to Wikipedia. Its originators claim there is a connection between neurological processes, language, and behavior, learned through experience. However, that behavior is not set in stone—it can be changed to achieve specific goals. It is said that NLP methodology can *model* the skills of exceptional people, allowing anyone to acquire them. Here are the three ways of communicating according to this methodology.

- **Visual** A picture is worth a thousand words, and by documenting your instructions, the team member has the tools to go back and review the process. For example, if you have a written process, set it up in a project management software system and include screenshots or pictures so that it will be easier for a visual learner to digest.

- **Auditory** An auditory person learns by hearing. Auditory learners may get frustrated when they have to read an instruction manual and may want someone else to explain it to them. They typically prefer audiobooks over printed or digital books.

- **Kinesthetic** A kinesthetic learner likes to feel and do things. For example, they may prefer to assemble a product or use a computer to search for information.

We learn with all three of these communication styles to some extent, but we usually have a dominant style. If you use all three styles to train, then you'll cover your bases with your employees. Your employees may know how they learn best, so ask them when they begin working with you—this will save you time and frustration. As you develop documented processes and procedures, consider using a combination of video, audio, and written documents so that each person can learn in their preferred style. Afterward, have employees give you feedback on what they heard. As they do, you'll recognize where their learning gaps are; this also gives them permission to ask for clarification.

The Competence Quadrant

Each person is at a different level of competence for each thing they're being asked to do.

- **Unconscious competence** is like getting behind the wheel of your car—you don't have to think about how to drive once you become proficient. You can talk or listen to the radio without thinking about driving. If you are unconsciously competent, you can vary the process or even eliminate steps for completing a task because you know the ultimate goal and how to get there.

- **Conscious competence** means you're aware of each step in the appropriate order. This level of self-awareness allows you to be a great teacher. I am not the best at this, so I hire self-starting problem-solvers. I like giving my employees the end result that I want them to achieve and let them figure out how to get it done, but I do meet with them regularly to ensure they're on track. It can be frustrating for people who are not self-starters and need hand-holding. So, how do you find employees who can run with your project successfully with little direction? Interestingly, I have found that people with food service training can be the best hires; they know how to manage multiple, competing priorities and can solve complex problems.

- **Conscious incompetence** describes people who know they don't know everything, but they're open to learning. They have an awareness that makes it easier to receive and process information. These employees have some experience and training prior to being hired.

- **Unconscious incompetence** occurs when someone doesn't know what they don't know. For example, some young people think they know more than they do but often need guidance and coaching to become aware of what they don't know. In the workspace, interns may have received education but not specific training.

I'd like to think I've become a better leader with my current company. The mistakes I made at my first company taught me the lessons I've shared in this chapter, and I hope they help you avoid experiencing the challenges of your design business.

Summary

- You're responsible for all results within your company.

- Fix the problem, not the blame.

- Say "help me understand" when you need to resolve a problem. It reduces resistance and ensures that the other person is open to correction.

- Expect to repeat instructions up to seven times for someone to hear what you said and process it.

- Incorporate the feedback loop after you've given instructions to ensure the other party understood what you said.

- Delegate instead of abdicating.

- Mentoring starts with explaining *why, what, how,* and *what if* (in that order).

- Communicate in the style in which each employee processes information—visual, auditory, or kinesthetic.

Finances

Few designers love finances because designers are typically right-brained. It doesn't mean they can't learn about finances, but it does mean that it may take some time to learn the basics. It's like a new language—it takes practice to understand something that seems alien to the way one thinks naturally. However, to run a great business, understanding finances is not optional.

Make a promise to yourself that you will learn this piece of the puzzle so that you can achieve financial freedom and confidence. You are capable!

Let's dig in….

CHAPTER 7

How Financially Successful Designers Charge for Their Services

You know your business is a commodity when prospects start the conversation by asking you about price.

—ALLAN DIB

Fees and markups are always challenging for our clients. They generally don't know how to price or sell their services or how to make money. It is an art form to find the right pricing for your unique business. Some of that comes from trial and error, and some comes from direct guidance from other experts.

If you are selling a pair of shoes for $20 and someone decides to buy them, they perceive the shoes to be worth more than what they paid or they wouldn't buy them. You're not forcing them to buy shoes—it's their choice. Thus, value exchange is win-win and based purely on perception.

Value is also subjective. If you offered that same person $20 for the shoes they just bought, they probably wouldn't sell them because they see them as worth more than $20. Even if you offered $30, they still might not sell them. There is no *correct* price for goods and services; it is instead the perceived value attributed to the product or service by each client. If the price is too high, the client won't exchange their money for it.

We are extremely lucky to live in a society with a system of money. It allows us to borrow, lend, and leverage our ability to scale. Our work would be enormously limited in a bartering and trading system. Earning money is a completely moral pursuit when it is done with honesty and integrity, but if you don't feel moral about the work you're doing, then you should probably change careers. When you believe in the value you provide, so much so that you feel you are doing people a disservice by not offering them your services, you're on track to creating massive value.

Our work should be a reflection of us. It's always the client's choice whether they perceive value in what we're offering or not.

Implementing a Fee Structure

If I want a full house for my speaking events, I talk about fees. It guarantees a standing-room-only crowd.

Because you're not attending a live event at this very moment, you get access to more information about fees than I can typically cover at a speaking event and valuable knowledge that will save you time and stress. (If you want more help, be sure to read through the end of this chapter to get access to our Easy Budget Calculator in our Profit & Pricing Shortcuts. You'll discover several ways to price your project. By just inputting a few numbers, you'll be able to create a budget in fifteen minutes or less.)

Does it ever seem that there are as many fee structures as there are design firms? So many possibilities lead to so much confusion when looking for answers to these extremely important, age-old questions:

- How do I charge and get clients to pay what I ask for and feel that I deserve?

- How do I get paid fairly for my services?

My intention is to offer guidance on the many choices out there, so when it comes time for you to charge for your services, you can make an informed decision.

When it comes to fee structures, designers make mistakes. I include myself in this sweeping generalization. For years I ran my own firm, and I made the same mistakes that many of you may be making today. The problem grew partly out of my incomplete design education, which did not teach us how to charge. In the one business class that was offered, the teacher talked about how designers charge in loose, undefined terms. Never once did they walk us through the pros and cons of each pricing option. Trial and error became my teacher; hopefully, this book will make certain that trial and error is not your main teacher.

Since so many designers don't love numbers or spreadsheets—and you may be one of them—get mentally ready to absorb the concepts. One thing I have witnessed in my coaching and consulting work is that the more comfortable you grow with numbers, the less you struggle to make money. The Easy Budget Calculator simplifies the process of pricing and tracking and, most important, making money as a designer. You can download the Easy Budget Calculator in our Profit & Pricing Shortcuts.

Though you may have started your firm as a way to enjoy your passion and make your clients' projects beautiful and functional, the purpose of business is to make money. Statistically, only 40 percent of businesses make a profit. I hope you're one of them, but if you're not (yet), avoiding mistakes is a great place to start shoring up your company.

One thought to bear in mind: You're a creative CEO who happens to provide design services. This is different than seeing yourself as a designer who happens to be charging for your services. Making that mind shift is a critical step toward greater financial success.

Fees are one aspect of creating a financially sustainable business. The rest depends on having a business model that connects your personal goals, vision, and values with a financial model that creates true value and profit. Your business is unique to you, so I won't tell you the best way to price your products and services, but by providing options for your pricing model, I believe you'll decide on the best way for you.

You can change your financial approach, have a profitable business, have happy clients, and enjoy the company you created. Breathe, relax, and read on—know that your path to profitability lies ahead!

Price Transparency

For so many years, price transparency has been a topic of conversation, not just for the design industry but across all industries. Price transparency is stating in clear terms to your client how you charge. For example, if you charge $150 per hour, mark up your products by 20 percent, and state that in your contract, then your client can see exactly how much you make.

Price transparency works for some designers but not for others. The reason? Client mindset. Some clients negotiate fees and markups because they simply don't want to pay for intangible services—they don't *appreciate the value* in the unseen services.

It's human nature to believe that creativity isn't valuable, and that's one reason there is so much conflict around large bills for time.

It's also human nature to want as much value as possible for the least amount of money, and if the client feels that you are overcharging them, they'll shop around. This is something that is true for even the most affluent clients, and it leads to the loss of trust and, potentially, the loss of a client.

Fee Options: The Road to Financial Freedom

You can choose from any of the following options to set up your fees. Which one you choose will depend on how you do business and how comfortable you are with discussing money with your clients.

Project Commitment

Many designers charge a retainer for their services. There's nothing wrong with asking for a retainer, but I think they'd be helping themselves by calling it a *project commitment*. With that name comes the implication that the client has a responsibility to pay you up front for your services. You want to use terms that convey the value of the service.

You never want to go into a contract without getting at least some money up front from your client. Think about your process. Now, specifically think about how much great value you are delivering on the front end of your projects. It's an astonishing amount, right? But what if you deliver services for up to thirty days without a project commitment? You may find that when your client gets your first bill, they won't pay it or go forward. This could mean several things:

- They weren't committed financially.
- You didn't set expectations well.
- Your contract wasn't fully reviewed with the client.

We suggest being very specific in your contract. Include how the project commitment is applied to your client's invoices. Hold on to the project commitment money until completion so that you always get paid for the last weeks of work that you do.

You should keep the project commitment fees in a reserve account because not all clients are ethical and fair, and those who aren't may withhold payment on the last bill as a negotiation tool to reduce the amount they pay you. Unethical clients will make excuses for why they shouldn't pay. (By the way, this isn't hypothetical; this has happened to me more than once—some of us have to repeatedly learn lessons.) Hopefully, you'll avoid this by following your ideal client dossier.

If you're in the fortunate position of having a waiting list (and I hope that you are!), use project commitment as a way for clients in your pipeline to secure a place on your calendar for future work. Give them homework to do each week so that they feel committed to working with you once you're available.

Hourly Only

Billing hourly only is an option that a handful of firms use. It entails passing their discounts directly onto clients without a markup and charging a higher hourly fee for all of their work. For example, if a designer typically charges $200 per hour, they double their fees to $400 per hour and charge for all work for the project. Hourly only is indeed an option; however, you have to know your cost structure and profit goal to be able to make enough money to sustain your business with an hourly fee.

Keep in mind that you risk losing the perception of value and services every time you send out an invoice. That's one reason why some people prefer to do fixed or value-based fees: You only have to sell the fees once.

Hourly rates today can range from $50 to $750 per hour. Principals always bill at the highest rate, but you can set up a tiered rate structure based on the level of experience of each team member.

If the client decides to purchase through your firm after the design and implementation phases, you can apply a percentage of the original fees you collected to product purchases. Here's something important to keep in mind if you choose this option: Reserve the percentage that you're willing to apply and keep it in a separate account so that you don't spend it prior to the completion of the job(s).

Hourly Plus Markup

Hourly plus markup is the most commonly used method of billing in design. Here, you must sell, meaning you must convince your clients as to why you bill by the hour and charge a markup on product every time you bill them. Trust me, when your client receives your proposals, they're doing the math each time to determine how much you're making—this can lead to conflict, negotiations, renegotiations, and a loss of trust.

Though complete transparency is preferred by some designers, it does open you up to negotiation by clients on your markups. You can also lose product sales, if the client shops you online—this behavior is growing more common every day. Even though your client may sign a letter of agreement, they may come back and negotiate later. This not only impacts your relationship with your client but also impacts your stress and frustration due to the loss of sales.

Markups typically range from 10 to 300 percent, depending on the type of product you're selling. Because of laws around price-fixing, we can't tell designers how to charge. You need to decide what works for you, based on the net profit margin you're trying to achieve. These formulas should help:

- Revenue – cost of goods sold – overhead = net profit $
- Net profit $/revenue $ = net profit margin %

Do you require that the client buy all their products from you? If so, be sure your contract includes information about how you deal with clients shopping you, then review all terms with the prospect at the time you present the contract. Finally, make sure you have them initial any phrases that have been problematic for you with previous clients.

Hourly Plus Discount from Manufacturer's Suggested Retail Price (MSRP)

Some designers prefer this method of billing because discounts vary, and if they buy through manufacturers and get stocking dealer prices, they can create higher margins. Beyond that, however, this method also gives the perception of saving money to your clients. Again, be sure to explain that you get compensated in two ways: billing for your time and your markup or profit on sales of products.

You earn your design fees for the intellectual property, creativity, experience, and vetted resources, and the markups or profits you add to your product cover the cost of executing the design concept and producing the beautiful end result.

Additionally, your markups also cover the cost of problem-solving when items are damaged (which we all know happens frequently), expediting (the more desirable phrase is *project management*), and profit for your business.

Discounts off of MSRP range from 10 to 25 percent, but what do you do if a vendor prices at net and doesn't indicate MSRP? Here is what we suggest:

- For fabric: At least double the net price.

- For furniture: Divide the net by at least 0.6—this will give you a typical furniture price offered by a showroom. For example, a $1,000 item ÷ 0.6 = $1,667 sale price.

  - A 10 percent discount = $1,500 sale price

    - $1,500 - $1,000 net cost = $500 profit

    - $500 ÷ $1,500 (sale price) = 33 percent profit margin

  - A 20 percent discount = $1,333 sale price

    - $1,333 - $1,000 net cost = $333 profit

    - $333 ÷ $1,333 (sale price) = 25 percent profit margin

- If you purchase at stocking dealer pricing, you may want to at least double the net price to arrive at a suggested MSRP.

Hourly Plus Specification Fee

In the section above, we covered hourly fees, but we have another option for you to consider—combining your hourly with a specification fee. Essentially, it's the same thing as a markup, but the reason you might like this better is because it gives you a more appealing way to explain it to your clients. For example: "Our specification fee covers the research, sourcing, and provision of specifications for purchasing. When we execute custom furnishings orders, it is important to hire someone who understands the complexities of them."

Another reason you might opt for this is because you can charge this fee even if you don't do the purchasing for the client. Your clients know that you're selecting products and providing purchasing information so they can buy them directly—they pay whether they buy from you or not. As always, please make sure this is clear in your contract, and also review it thoroughly with your client.

Fixed or Value-Based Fees

A simple definition will help clarify these terms: *fixed* or *value-based* fees are fees that you *sell* one time. With this fee option, your clients have clarity about how much they'll have to pay you for the entire project.

In highly competitive markets, fees and hourly rates are often so low that some designers struggle to make money. What we've come to understand by analyzing fixed or value-based fees is that designers typically underprice themselves by 50 percent, compared to what they would have earned had they billed by the hour. That is an extremely large percentage, which represents an equally large loss for the designer.

So, why use this method if you're likely to lose money? Sometimes designers base their fees on what they think the client will pay and, sadly, this is determined without regard for what they need to make to earn a great profit. Below is a review of how some designers calculate their fees, along with our honest opinion on the merit of each option.

- **Picking a number from thin air** Not advised!

- **A square footage price that is often randomly picked** This is not a good business practice, unless you have solid data (benchmarks) from past projects.

- **A detailed line-item spreadsheet** This is tedious and not advised, except when checking your numbers. The scope of a job often changes once you're under contract, so spending hours up front may be a waste of time if you don't get the job.

- **Benchmarking your projects** This means that you track your time and keep track of what you charge for typical rooms or projects. Make sure to check that you actually made money on every project. We highly recommend benchmarking so you can easily ballpark the project costs when asked by your clients and prospects. Always provide a range—being able to answer questions about budget parameters easily gives your clients and prospects confidence in your knowledge and professionalism.

- **A percentage of the project cost** For example, your fees could be 20 to 40 percent of the project cost. For a $100,000 project, the fee could be anywhere from $20,000 to $40,000. Again, your experience and knowledge of your actual percentage will help you estimate fees with confidence, and that will give clients confidence in you.

The biggest advantage of a fixed or value-based fee is clear: You only have to sell the fee one time. But to get the full picture of a fixed or value-based fee, you also need to see its biggest disadvantages.

- If you don't track your time and set time budgets for your team, you can easily run over the fee and lose money.

- It's human nature not to track the project scope, and things can get added by you or the client that don't get billed. Be careful to have a checklist for each project and give the client an addendum prior to working on additional scope. Otherwise, you're likely to be doing a lot of work for free.

- The fees can be so high that the client could choose not to work with you because of sticker shock, or you could end up negotiating your fees down and working for a much lower effective hourly rate than your stated rates.

Be sure to use our Easy Budget Calculator (included in the Profit & Pricing Shortcuts) so that you don't underprice your fixed or value-based fee.

Time Blocks

Some designers sell blocks of time and do so for a very specific reason: to gain commitment from their clients and give them peace of mind that they aren't going to get overwhelmed with large time bills. Some designers, for example, offer ten- to fifty-hour blocks. They keep the client informed about how many hours they've used on a regular basis.

One benefit to time blocks as a fee option is that it provides you with a great way to get started with a new client, and it gives them certainty that you won't continue to bill them without their approval.

Square Footage

Square footage is often the preferred choice when working on commercial projects or with builders, but it can also be used for decorating projects. Two things to keep in mind if you opt for square footage for your company:

- Specifications for new construction tend to be on the low end of the range from $1 to $10 per square foot.

- When using square footage for luxury decorating projects, prices can range from $500 to $1,000 per square foot for furnishings budgets.

Room Fee

For years, designers in New York City and other markets offered a fee per room, and the pricing varied dramatically. This could be $49 for a room in smaller markets and tens of thousands of dollars per room in higher-end, larger markets. Within the last few years, low fees per room were popularized by online companies that hired inexpensive *designers* to do projects for pennies. Thankfully, most of those companies disappeared a few years ago.

A good reason for using design fees per room is that it allows you to bring in a modest amount of quick cash. While there's no denying the benefit of quick cash (at times), the bigger point to consider is that the room fee model is not a strong, long-term strategy for growing a highly profitable and enduring business if the numbers don't really compensate for your team's time.

The fee-per-room model requires a *churn and burn* orientation. Fees are typically so low that they attract low-end clients who don't place value on luxury design services and just want to buy their own products to save money. Although many big companies with venture capital behind them adopted this pricing strategy in the past, they weren't terribly successful with it, perhaps because the designers working for them were paid too little money to do fast-paced projects.

In spite of their failure, it is possible to earn some revenue from this type of model. There are well-known designers who charge huge room fees, in some instances over $50,000.

As with all the strategies we've laid out, it's up to you to decide if this is the one for you. A large part of that decision comes from understanding what you want your brand to represent in the marketplace.

Percentage of Project

Charging a percentage of a project typically happens on new construction or ultra-luxury design. At one of our annual Genius Exchange events, a New York-based celebrity designer shared that he often bills 23 to 27 percent of the cost of a project for managing it. Additionally, he noted that he charges a room fee, plus a markup on product. His body of work and his remarkable reputation allow him to command multimillion-dollar fees and markups; he has worked incredibly hard over many years to secure the position he owns within the industry.

Hybrid Fees

Another approach to consider for billing is charging a design fee for the first phases of the project, then switching to a percentage of the overall budget, or even hourly billing. The reason behind a hybrid approach makes sense for some: fixed fees don't always work for the middle phase of a project, particularly when many job site visits are required, and the scope of work often changes daily.

Another way to bill is to establish a fixed fee but bill a set amount per month for the expected duration of the project. The two things you need to factor in if you adopt this option are:

- Managing the cash flow during the early phases of the project, when the majority of design time occurs.

- Spreading out the cash flow so that you don't end up collecting large chunks of money up front, spending it, and running out of money toward the end of the project. Keep this thought in mind: If you do collect large, fixed fees up front or early in the project, it's critical to remember that you haven't earned that money until you've billed or logged time against it. Just because you have a large amount of money in your bank account does not mean that you can spend that cash. You need to know how much of that money is yours to spend.

Reimbursables

Reimbursables, such as blueprints, expedited shipping, freight, delivery, installation, mileage, and miscellaneous expenses, can be billed, which is a reassuring thought. But it's up to you to decide what expenses you will bill for, as opposed to those you decide to absorb into your other fees or markups. Clients hate being nickeled-and-dimed—there is a cost of paying reimbursable expenses on your behalf. For example, you have to pay your bookkeeper, then you wait to be paid by the client. Therefore, you should charge a markup on any significant reimbursables. Ten to fifteen percent is typical.

Travel

Some designers bill a per diem for travel. They calculate their hourly rate and either charge a half or full rate for the day times eight hours, plus travel costs. It makes sense to set a certain amount of money aside for each meal, such as $15 for breakfast, $25 for lunch, and $35 for dinner, and miscellaneous expenses, like bottled water and coffee. If you like wine or cocktails, that should not be billed to the client.

Rounding your per diem travel expenses to $150 to $200 per day, including baggage fees and tips, makes it easy for you, the client, and your team. You might also consider billing $1,000 to $1,500 for travel, if you are flying in for a day and one night. This should include all transportation, food, and incidentals. Billing separately for transportation and hotel costs, plus 15 percent, lets you cover the internal costs of accounting. Otherwise, you can let your client purchase tickets and pay for travel directly to the providers. Some clients provide a low limit on a credit card for the designer for travel and incidentals.

Depending on where you live, you might find yourself spending a great deal of time in your car going to and from a client's home or office. If you know this will be the case, consider billing portal-to-portal. Doing this is easy: You start the clock when you leave your office, and you stop the clock when you return to it. This can be done in lieu of billing for mileage and charging a half rate.

In places like Los Angeles, you could drive half a day, every day, so it's crucial that you recapture the non-design time that's associated with serving that client.

Markup of Subcontractor or Contractor Fees

Please check state laws because some states, like California and Florida, don't allow you to mark up subcontractor fees. Also, if you do charge a markup, these states will consider you to be a contractor, so if you're not licensed as a general contractor, you can get in trouble for using this billing practice. It does put you in an implied position of being a general contractor, so wherever your design firm is located, it's best practice to research your state's laws. If you can, by law, mark up subcontractor fees— the typical range is 16 to 20 percent.

Evergreen Retainer

When you have a retainer that your client refreshes as the balance drops to a certain level, you are using an *evergreen retainer*. For example, if you collect $10,000 and you bill $5,500 against it, you bill for replenishment of $5,500 on your next invoice.

Administrative Fee, or Administrative, Installation, and Delivery Fees

If you don't charge for your time during the purchasing phase, you might consider charging an administrative fee of 2 to 10 percent in addition to your markup or discount from MSRP. This allows you to cover the cost of your accounting services and team time, as well as your delivery costs.

Building Materials

Some designers mark up building materials. If you decide to do this, you may cross a line that puts you in a general contractor role. Depending upon the state you're in, doing this could put you at risk for penalties, lawsuits, and fines. Beyond that, however, it can also put you in an adversarial position with builders or contractors because that's how they make their money. When considering this fee option, think carefully about whether it is worth risking a happy relationship with the trades.

Freight for Commercial Projects

Depending on the type of work you're doing, adding a percentage markup to freight may not be allowed. You may need to do a straight pass-through of the actual invoiced expense.

When creating your fee structure, remember to always use a contract and be very thorough to ensure you have no grey areas that could lead to conflict with your client. Review your contract with the client for things that cause—or could potentially cause—conflict, and don't forget to have your client acknowledge their approval by initialing for potential problem clauses.

Summary

- Plan for your personal financial goals first so you know how much money your business must generate to achieve your overall goals.

- If you aren't confident with how you bill and how you *sell* your fees, you will run into problems. These can be avoided if you decide which of the options above works best for you, your brand, and the life you want to lead. Once you do that, all you have to do is script your conversations and practice, practice, practice.

- We occasionally host 5-Day Financial Blueprint Challenges, so if you struggle with earning what you deserve, please be sure to subscribe to be notified of these events.

- Be sure to get access to our free Profit & Pricing Shortcuts, including our Easy Budget Calculator.

CHAPTER 8

Understanding Financials

The only way you grow is by being uncomfortable.
—SCOTT HARRIS

Understanding financials is like having blood in your veins—it is essential to your survival. Even if you have been told you aren't good with numbers (yet!), let me help you understand the essentials. Since you are unlikely to have a business degree, why would you know how to read financial statements? It isn't something that is taught in most creative degree programs, but when planning on running a business, it's important to be open to the possibility that you can learn.

Ban Negative Beliefs

Waving a hand over her head, Kim, who is an architect, told me that her eyes glaze over when she looks at her financial statements. I'll tell you what I told her—you're flying blind if you're operating a business without understanding the following:

- Your balance sheet
- Your income statement (aka your profit and loss statement, or P&L)
- Your cash flow forecast

Financial Statement #1: The Balance Sheet (Past)

I describe the balance sheet as all financial results that have happened from the date you started your business to this exact moment in time. The balance sheet tracks all transactions that haven't been billed yet or have been billed and haven't been paid by your client. For simplicity, let's think of it as your financial history.

Rather than get into a lot of detail here, for now you just need to understand the principal purpose of your balance sheet. It tells you what financial items may be in a holding pattern. Here are some formulas to help you further understand its mechanics.

- Assets = liabilities + shareholder's equity: This equation balances, thus it is called the balance sheet.

- If you own a home, the asset (aka home) value – mortgage = your home equity. Your business equity is the equivalent of your home equity.

- Shareholder's equity = the net worth of your business after all debts are paid.

A balance sheet consists of three parts:

Assets Think of assets like the value of your house on Zillow. Current assets are financial accounts that can be liquidated in less than a year to pay expenses and debts. They commonly include the following:

- **Checking account balance(s)** I recommend having one account to pay your business operating expenses and a second account to pay vendors for products and services.

- **Savings account balance(s)** You should have one account for taxes and one for emergencies.

- **Accounts receivable** If you haven't been paid in full on an invoice you've sent to the client, the balance due shows up in accounts receivable.

- **Work in progress** What you've paid to vendors on behalf of your clients.

- **Long-term assets** These can include things like inventory, vehicles, buildings, office equipment, furniture, leasehold improvements, and accumulated depreciation.

Liabilities These are items that you owe. For example, client deposits are funds that you received for items that haven't been invoiced. Until you invoice for products delivered, you still owe the client delivery of what they paid for. Until then, you are liable for the money you collected for those items. Think of liabilities like your mortgage on your house. Current liabilities are bills that you will pay in less than a year and can include:

- **Accounts payable** This includes things like supplies and so on.

- **Sales tax payable** Note that this should never be shown on your P&L because you collect sales tax from your client on behalf of the state or city. When you pay the sales tax, it reduces your liability on the balance sheet. Other taxes, like federal, state, and local taxes, may also be shown as a liability on your balance sheet.

- **Credit cards**

- **Auto loans**

For every $1 of current liabilities, you want to have at least $1 of current assets—a ratio of 1:1 is your minimum goal. I'd prefer that you have $2 of current assets to every $1 of current liabilities; if you can, set that as your goal.

Long-term liabilities can include:

- Car loans

- Lines of credit to help you through cash flow cycles

- A mortgage on a building

- Other loans, such as an SBA loan, for the operation of your business

Equity Equity is the value of your business after the deduction of liabilities from assets. Typical shareholders' equity categories may include:

- **Common stock** If you're set up as a corporation, there is usually some value assigned to the shares of stock.

- **Paid in capital** For example, this may be your initial investment to start the company.

- **Shareholder contributions** Additional money you invested in the company after inception.

- **Shareholder distributions (aka draws)** What you've withdrawn from your bank and paid to yourself for taxes or personal expenses.

- **Retained earnings** What you've earned in net profit over your years in business.

- **Net profit or loss** This is for the current year.

Note: Do not draw more cash out of your business than what is shown in retained earnings or you could end up bankrupting your company.

Financial Statement #2: Profit and Loss, aka P&L or Income Statement (Present)

The title of this financial statement may be named differently, depending on the accounting software you use. The three terms above are interchangeable.

Your P&L may be for an entire fiscal year—you may have started your business on a date other than January 1, so it would be for a full fiscal year from the start date (i.e., April 1, 2030, to March 31, 2031). It can also cover a calendar year, for the month to date, or for a full month of any year. Depending on your access to the accounting software program you use, you can hopefully run your P&L at any time.

Your accounting software may be run on an *accrual* or *cash* basis. Accrual basis describes revenues and expenses recorded when they are incurred, regardless of when cash is received or paid to vendors or suppliers. Cash basis means that revenues and expenses are recorded when cash is received or paid to vendors or suppliers. Most design-oriented accounting software is run on an accrual basis; however, your CPA may adjust your P&L to a cash basis for tax purposes. (We are not bookkeepers, CPAs, CFOs, or tax experts, so please confirm all financial details with experts.)

There are three main parts of a P&L:

- **Revenue (aka sales or income)** This is what your client pays you for what has been invoiced:

  - Product sales

  - Time billing (aka fees)

  - Commissions paid to you

  - Sales tax fee (for your collecting sales tax on behalf of your taxing authority)

  - Freight

  - Crating

  - Installation

  - Delivery

  - Reimbursable expenses like airfare, mileage, meals, hotels, etc.

- **Cost of goods sold (aka COGS, cost of sales, or COS)** What you pay to vendors or subcontractors for the goods or services you sell, which is shown as revenue. Typical categories might include:

  - Cost of goods (furniture, fabric, etc.)
  - Freight expenses
  - Crating expenses
  - Installation expenses

Note that you should have a corresponding COGS category for every revenue category (i.e., product sales, furniture and COGS, furniture). The only exception is time billing since payroll paid to produce time billing is found in the third section of the P&L.

- **Overhead (aka administrative expenses or expenses)** This includes all items that you must pay, whether you have $1 in sales or not. The expenses in these categories may include fixed expenses like insurance or rent and variable expenses like travel, meals, and so on. Here are some examples of typical expense categories:

  - Advertising, marketing, and public relations
  - Auto expenses
  - Dues and subscriptions
  - Education
  - Insurance
  - Interest expenses
  - Legal and professional fees
  - Meals
  - Mileage
  - Office supplies

- Payroll

- Printing

- Rent

- Repairs and maintenance

- Software

- Telephone

- Travel

- Utilities

And finally, after all of your COGS and overhead expenses are paid, the remainder is called *net profit* or *net loss*. Your net profit is the same as your *bottom line* before you take draws or pay taxes. Be very careful not to take all of the net profit out of the business each year because you need to save money for the following:

- **Income tax** It is often a draw that you take out of your checking to pay for estimated taxes.

- **Money for future growth (aka reserves)** You should shoot for between three and six months of total overhead expenses, or you may want to save enough to weather a year of difficult financial times.

Note 1: A good rule of thumb is to draw out only 25 to 50 percent of your net profit per year for your personal use.

Note 2: Take 10 percent of every check or payment you receive from a client and put it into a savings account for reserves.

Financial Statement #3: Cash Flow Statement (Future)
Now that we've reviewed your balance sheet and P&L, it is time to review what you can anticipate receiving or paying in the future. This statement allows you to predict future sales, as well as your cash position.

Typically, you start with a cash balance in your checking or savings account. For example, let's say you have $100,000 in all of your accounts combined. From this total, you'll want to predict any cash that will be collected or paid out in future months.

Cash in can come from a number of different sources:

- Time billing by client
- Product deposits, sales tax, freight, etc., paid by the client
- Commissions
- Refunds
- Other fees

Cash out may be for:

- Product deposits or balances due
- Overhead expenses like rent, payroll, etc.
- Payments for liabilities, such as loans, lines of credit, mortgages, and credit cards
- Bonuses
- Commissions
- Owners' draws
- Taxes

You have either positive or negative cash flow each month. All businesses experience variations—just know that cash flow won't always be positive. It only matters that your projections are mostly positive for future months. If they are not, you need guidance on what to do to fix any financial problems you may have.

Budgeting

Sadly, less than 10 percent of the designers we coach or consult with come to us with a budget. Because of this, they have inconsistent financial results. I'm more concerned with a firm having a budget than a business plan, since few people actually read their business plan once they write it.

At the very least, put together an annual budget every November so that you're ready to tackle your year with clarity around the following:

- Revenue you need per month to achieve your goals of income and profit. It's especially important that you know your typical job size so that you can figure out how many jobs you'll need per month.

- Can you afford to hire and give raises or bonuses?

- Can you add benefits like health insurance or a 401(k)?

- Can you give yourself a raise?

- Are you expensing everything possible that is allowed by the IRS to reduce your net profit?

- Expected profit

- Future expansion needs. For example, will you be opening an office, moving your office, buying equipment or furniture, and so on?

Financial Rules of Thumb

Review all three financial statements at least once a month with your bookkeeper. Have your bookkeeper give you a quick summary of the following data on a weekly, if not daily, basis:

- Current assets (at minimum, checking, savings, and accounts receivable)

- Current liabilities (credit cards, sales tax, other taxes, and any bills due in less than a year)

- The number and dollar amount of unpaid invoices over thirty days past invoice date

- Hours billed by the team

Also, (this bears repeating) remember to save 10 percent of each check or credit card payment received by each client, and don't draw more than 25 to 50 percent of net profit during any given year so that you'll always have money in reserve.

Meet with your CPA to review estimated sales for the quarter and for the year so that you stay current with your income taxes. Keep your cash flow projection up to date each month, and shoot for having a full pipeline of projects for at least three months ahead.

As I explained the three key financial statements we discussed in this chapter during Kim's second VIP Day, the lightbulb finally went on, and she was moved to tears. Within a year, she had won our Entrepreneur of the Year award for growth and profit.

You can do what Kim did. Refer to this chapter and the glossary at the end of the book until you understand these financial terms without thinking about them. Then you can finally ban any negative thoughts that say "I can't understand the numbers of my business." You can learn to read and understand financials, I promise!

Summary

- You're flying blind if you're operating a business without understanding your financial statements. Wouldn't you prefer to know how to run your business and make a profit so that you can achieve financial freedom?

- Your financial future depends on the continued bottom-line (net profit) growth of your business. When looking at your balance sheet, pay attention to your retained earnings so that you don't draw too much out of it.

- You want to increase your revenue every year, but more importantly, you want to increase your net profit on your income statement. The industry average for the net profit of interior designers is less than 8 percent. We help our clients at least double that; this should also be your goal.

- The cash flow forecast is my favorite financial statement. I hope it becomes yours as well. Always stay informed about how much business is in your pipeline, and **always market when you are busiest** so that you have a full pipeline as you finish big projects.

CHAPTER 9

Planning for Profit

*If you don't know where you're going…
any road will take you there.*

—LEWIS CARROLL, ALICE IN WONDERLAND

Planning for profit is essential, and pricing is just one element of ensuring profitability. Perhaps you've held the belief that increasing sales and revenue (what you get paid for your services and products) will guarantee that you will make more money. This belief is not always true!

There is a saying that "revenue is vanity; profit is sanity." Making more money should indicate that you are keeping more of what you brought into your business. That means profit. Increasing revenue and the cost of materials (i.e., the cost of goods sold) purchased, with an increase in overhead, could just as easily lead to you losing money. It's important to adjust the right dials at the right time to ensure that you're keeping more money at any point in time.

Striking a Balance to Increase Net Profit

During a VIP Day with Andrea, we had a discussion about her net profit. After I took a look at her P&L, it was clear that she needed a different plan. Money is typically emotional for business owners, and that was certainly the case with Andrea. She burst into tears as we noted her profit was minimal, especially considering how hard she worked.

Although Andrea could read and understand her financial statements, she didn't know exactly what to do to increase her net profit. She did her best every day to sell more clients and products, manage her team, and put one foot in front of the other, but nothing was working to move the bottom line higher. She was in debt and stressed, particularly as she was the primary breadwinner in her family.

Before she became a designer, Andrea was a pharmaceutical sales rep making over $100,000 a year. She was now making far less, and her husband questioned if she could continue running her own business. She often wondered if she had done the right thing by giving up such a high-paying job to do what she loved. She wanted to know what to do to change her financial situation.

Having reserves and paying oneself well is a right that all business owners have. You deserve to earn a great living because you work even harder than someone who has a job. You spend time away from your family and friends working to make your clients happy, and you put your own financial future at risk every day that you run a business.

Having the right balance of billable and non-billable employees and looking at each line item on your P&L to ensure that it is essential is just a small part of budgeting effectively.

So, how much should you be charging per hour to make money on your designers? It depends on how productive your employees are.

It's also important to understand the real cost of having an employee on your team. *Burden* means the cost of having employees, plus their salaries. For example, your burden for having employees includes covering their insurance, 401(k), cell phone reimbursement, and so on. For billable employees, you should be billing at least three to four times their burdened rate.

Another rule of thumb is that your owner's salary should be 10 to 20 percent of your revenue. So, if you're bringing in a million dollars in revenue, you should be earning at least $100,000 to $200,000 per year before net profit. If you didn't earn that percentage, then why not? Look at your numbers or meet your bookkeeper to figure out where the leaks are in your financial model.

Assessing Your Needs

The percentage of net profit you should earn depends on the size of your business. Though the industry's average net profit in 2020 was under 8 percent, we set goals for our clients to earn between 10 and 25 percent net profit after their salary.

If you don't have a budget, you're not alone. As mentioned, most of our VIP clients didn't have one when they first met with us, but we helped them put together a three-year financial model during their VIP Experience™. If you have financial goals, you need to manage your activities to achieve them.

In my businesses, I've always used our budget as the cornerstone of our strategic plan. Let's do an exercise together to figure out yours:

- How much revenue do you want to bring in during your next calendar year? _____

- What is the average size of project that you typically get? _____

- Divide your desired revenue by your average project size: _____

- Now, divide the number of clients needed by twelve to calculate how many projects you need per month to hit your goal. _____

For example, if your project size is typically $5,000 and you want to make $500,000 in revenue, then you'll need 100 clients during the year, or two per week, to achieve your sales goal. Better yet, if you typically do

$50,000 projects and have the same revenue goal, you'll only need ten clients for the year, or less than one new project per month.

It's important to remember that not all leads are the same—some are ideal, and some are not. I count ideal leads versus total contacts (via email or phone). You want to close at least 20 percent or, even better, more than 60 percent of your qualified leads.

Let's say you get ten calls per month. Out of those ten, five are qualified leads, meaning that they're doing the types of projects you prefer. Let's look at the math:

- Five out of ten = 50 percent of leads are qualified

- Five times a 20 percent close rate = one new client acquired

- Five times a 50 percent close rate = two and a half new clients acquired

If you're closing 50 percent of the inquiries from qualified clients and you have a full pipeline, it's time to raise your fees. Even charging a few more dollars per hour can make a big difference to your bottom line.

During our VIP Days, we teach a process we call the Bottom-Up Budget Calculator. I encourage you to try it below. Your total compensation as an owner includes the following:

- **Owner's salary** The salary you pay yourself out of your P&L each month. (If you are set up as an LLC, you typically draw from your net profit to pay yourself. If you operate as an S-Corp, the IRS wants you to pay yourself a reasonable salary and withhold social security taxes before you draw out additional net profit.)

- **Perks** These could be things like auto expenses, insurance, cell phone, travel, meals, etc. that you pay yourself out of your business.

- **Net profit** This also counts as owner's compensation because you pay taxes on it.

Decide what percentage of bottom-line profit you want to earn. For the purposes of this exercise, let's say you plan to earn a 10 percent net profit after paying for COGS and overhead. Divide 100 percent by 10 percent and that equals the multiplier you need to figure out how much revenue you must bring in for the year.

Let's say you want to earn $100,000 in net profit for the year. Multiply $100,000 times the multiplier of 10. This equals $1,000,000 in revenue that you need to bring in if you want to earn a 10 percent net profit. If you want to earn $100,000 in net profit and your desired percentage of profit is 20 percent, then divide 100 percent by 20 percent. This gives you a multiplier of five. Therefore, you need to bring in $500,000 of revenue ($100,000 times five) to earn a $100,000 net profit.

What Is Your Profit Margin?

Net margin is a percentage of net profit dollars divided by revenue dollars. As an example, $100,000 net profit divided by $500,000 revenue equals a 20 percent net margin.

There are several ways to increase your net profit dollars (and net margin percentage), and you can do one or all of these together:

- Raise your hourly rates
- Bill more hours
- Hire more billable employees
- Increase your markup
- Cut COGS by buying at stocking dealer pricing
- Decrease overhead costs

It's pretty simple to make more money if you do all of the above. The biggest obstacle is typically the owner's fear of raising rates or markups; however, if you want to make more money, you must ensure that you're turning all of the dials even one percentage point or $1. It will make a big difference in what you earn for the bottom line.

This bears repeating: even if you have a healthy bank account (some of which is your client's product money), do *not* spend all of your net profit! Make sure you have enough money set aside for taxes and reserves in your business. (Forgive me for saying this again!) Plan to draw only 25 to 50 percent of your net profit per year and you'll have a healthy and sustainable business.

Margin Versus Markup

There is a big difference between margin and markup, and most designers don't know this distinction.

A *markup* is what you add to the net cost you pay to a vendor; it is used to calculate the sale price of your goods. Markups are shown on proposals. For example, if a $100 pillow with a 50 percent markup equates to $50 in profit, you will earn from selling the pillow. A $100 net cost plus a $50 profit equals a $150 sale price to the client.

A *margin* only shows up on your P&L. For example, your revenue for the pillow is $150 and your COGS is $100. A $50 profit divided by a $150 sale price equals a 33 percent margin. It is important to understand that a margin is the percentage of profit you are earning on the sale. You can't earn a markup on a sale.

MARK-UP	MARGIN
10%	9.09%
15%	13.04%
20%	16.70%
25%	20.00%
30%	23.08%
35%	25.90%
40%	28.60%
43%	30.00%
45%	31.03%
50%	33.00%
55%	35.50%
60%	37.50%
100%	50.00%
200%	67.00%
300%	75.00%

In the interior design industry, with the cost of operating and paying your team, we suggest that you charge at least a 30 percent markup.

In one year, Andrea went from being in debt to having cash reserves and a 4249 percent increase in net profit. She is now on track to reaching her personal financial goals.

In principle, it's great to know how to read a P&L statement, but what really matters is understanding how to make more money. Now you know how.

Summary

- Having billable employees on your team is how you make money. You need enough employees generating money to offset non-billable employees, such as your bookkeeper or business manager.

- Knowing how to create a budget isn't taught in design school, but learning to do so is a wonderful thing! (See the Bottom-Up Budget Calculator exercise.)

- Track your numbers every month—at a minimum, you should review your P&L, balance sheet, and cash flow statement.

- For extra credit, track how many leads you're getting each month. Note how many of those are qualified and ideal clients and, of those, how many you typically close. With that information, you can achieve your personal financial goals more easily.

Marketing, Mindset, and Mastery of Yourself

Marketing is the lifeblood of your business. Without consistent and relentless marketing, your lead flow will be insufficient and stress-inducing. Learn to love marketing. It's essential to your success.

As I mentioned earlier in the book, the reason why most businesses experience wild swings in revenue is due to not marketing when they're the busiest. It's essential that you market consistently, especially when you can barely breathe from the heavy workload. Marketing at the precise moment of overwhelm fills the future pipeline so your revenue swings are less terrifying. Waiting until your pipeline is nearly empty to market is a recipe for stress and potential business failure.

Keep in mind that just because I say that you need to market doesn't mean that you, as the owner, have to do all of the work. You just need to plan and delegate or outsource the marketing process.

Mindset is so important that I'll highlight additional shifts you might want to consider as you get ready to apply the ideas of this book. With courage, confidence, decisiveness, and action, your business will reach levels you never imagined. Dream big and commit to mastering the skills and mindset that will transform your business and your life.

CHAPTER 10

Marketing Is an Inside-Out Job

What you offer is not just your product. Your offering is product, services, your employees, your experiences, your ideas, your other customers, and even your competitors. So, sell them all. When you are good at what you do, the product or service you offer is just the way people build the first link to you. It's the top of a huge pyramid. But the base of the pyramid, the real service, is when customers have access to you, and you can provide advice and the full power of your network and experience. This is when you are over-delivering on steroids and how you build real wealth—not just a one-time fee for a service or product.

—JAMES ALTUCHER

One of our clients, Barbara, started with us when she was pregnant with her second child. She wasn't working full-time, but she had three employees, two of whom were part-time. She came to us because she wanted to figure out how to scale her business. Barbara was a step ahead of where some people are when they are just starting out. She already had a well-defined style and a great head for business; she just needed to know how to create her financial model and understand the key money drivers of her company.

What you need to focus on in Phase 1 of your business—during what we call your Business Breakthrough—is proving to yourself, your family, and your clients that you're worthy of charging for your talent. (You do know that you are worthy of earning a great living as a designer, right?) You may need to work through some limiting beliefs that could slow your progress. As Wall Street advisor Geoff Blades says, "Timid salespeople have hungry kids." There's no time like the present to market yourself—always be marketing.

Most designers I know rely on inbound marketing (i.e., referrals) or they procrastinate about marketing because they don't know how to get clients without being salesy or pushy. They may even feel uncomfortable asking for referrals. Disliking the process of acquiring clients is a recipe for a low income—while waiting for the next great prospect to call, you'll be at the mercy of a stomach-twisting revenue roller coaster. During the early growth period of your business, you will get the most mileage out of your connections or what we call *relationship marketing*.

Relationship Marketing

Attracting and signing the right clients is a fundamental requirement of running a successful business, and as your company grows, the level of projects and the revenue from those projects will increase. For most firms, the process of going to the *next level* is organic, but you can also increase your company's speed of growth by developing a clear marketing strategy and tactical plan.

Mindset also can't be understated here—it is the key to growing your business more quickly. When you're in the early stages of getting established, it feels as if you are doing everything—and you are! I promise, it will get better.

Right after I graduated from design school, my husband and I moved to a tired house in a great neighborhood in Denver so we could live close to the types of clients I wanted to serve. We remodeled the house before we moved in and continued to improve upon it over the course of our first year of living in the neighborhood.

After we finished the remodel, we hosted an open house for our neighbors as a way to get to know them. During the party, a neighbor at the end of the block said she needed help with blinds in her master bathroom. That conversation turned into a multi-six-figure project over the course of the next few years. After we completed the project, she and her husband bought several homes in multiple states.

During the early stages of your business, your home can be your launching pad. If you have a knack for renovating and you want to do remodeling as a regular part of your business, host a *before* party followed by an *after*-party. Your neighbors will love it! Don't forget to invite Realtors who live and work in your area—this will also lead to referrals.

In the early stages of my design business, I also worked for friends at reduced rates. Before long, my friends paid full rates because I discovered that they were my most challenging clients. They expected the most service and the best deals and demanded more attention; however, they knew this about themselves, so they were willing to pay the full rate. I found that if I didn't charge them the same rate as I charged my other clients, I felt underpaid and I could only be mad at myself.

In the first few years of the business, I remember sitting in my office thinking about how to build my client list. I brainstormed for the better part of a day on how to get the right kinds of clients with great budgets. (You might want to do this, too.) I created my vision for the types of projects that I wanted to do and thought about how to meet the people who would hire me for those projects. Very quickly, it became clear that I needed to expand my network of acquaintances.

My Top Ten Marketing Priorities

During my first five years of business, these were my marketing priorities:

- **Showing my own work and hosting parties for neighbors, Realtors, and friends** This worked well for me and resulted in many lucrative projects.

- **Working with friends and family and hosting after-parties at their homes** This was always effective for me. We hosted charity events, and after-parties were always a big hit.

- **Referrals** Most designers build their business on referrals, especially in the early stages. It is important to have a plan around getting them—you should ask every client to refer you if they're happy with the work that you've done. When you sign a contract with them, let them know that you grow your business by referrals and remind them again when the project is completed. The best time to ask for a referral is when your clients are the happiest, so *reveal days* can be perfect for providing a lookbook or gift card for your client to give to their friends.

- **Charitable organizations** I took the top Denver Realtor, Edie, and her husband to dinner and asked them about their involvement in the community and recommendations for the best places to get involved. At that time, I didn't ask her for referrals; the dinner was to get to know her and vice versa. It took three years, but she started referring me to her buyers and I landed several multi-six-figure projects as a result of her friendship.

- **Realtors** Edie was a great resource for leads, but several other Realtors also referred us over time. I got to know the brokers of several firms and dropped off gifts and provided educational sessions and even gift certificates to their buyers. I would also go out to meet with their clients to see if certain houses could be renovated to suit their needs. Doing this helped me get quite a few projects.

- **Builders** I made a point to reach out to several builders. Five years into the business, we added a designer to run our construction finishes department. That generated furnishings revenue for us, and it was a great way to get repeat referrals.

- **Contractors** I joined a local remodelers' organization and got to know several contractors I worked with or who referred work to me.

- **Architects** I got to know a few and even renovated a home for one of my architect friends.

- **Photographers** You need to photograph your work, so be sure to hire the best photographer you can afford. If they are connected to a magazine, you can get published easily because magazines have slim budgets for photography. They already know the editors, so that's a shortcut to getting published.

- **Editors and writers** I got to know the editor of *Colorado Homes & Lifestyle* magazine and wrote articles for them. Our local newspapers also had home sections, which generated more press for me.

As you can see, I was motivated and determined to grow my business. Every day I marketed, and every day I got leads. The marketing work that I did was consistent; I had more time than money, so I focused on relationship building, which will also serve you well in your business.

Be Fearless, Even if You Don't Feel Fearless

Building a business means influencing and convincing prospects to work with you over other designers. Confidence is a necessary success tool, and the only way you become confident is to decide what to do and get into action. Often, the confidence comes after you are courageous.

Many designers love the work they do, but they are nervous about working with affluent clients, especially if they aren't in the same social circles. That doesn't matter—what matters is who you are deep inside and how talented you are. If you're a great businessperson who loves to market, you can be more successful than some of the most talented designers in your area.

If you can't communicate with confidence, it will be harder to ask for referrals. However, you may find that your clients will willingly promote you if you wow them with your service, so if you're shy about self-promotion, then just focus on wowing your clients.

Ultra-affluent clients may not refer you, and that can be disappointing. They also may not allow you to take photographs of their project for security reasons. Just know that privacy and confidentiality are very important with these clients.

Your style will evolve over time, which is essential to attract bigger and more desirable projects. With each job, you will learn to be a better designer by honing your preferences for what you think is beautiful, and you will also learn to be a better businessperson. You will develop a clear identity for yourself, your work, and the business you want to build. Allow all of these elements to evolve and unfold—it's part of the beauty of creating your own business. A brand is you at your core expressed to the world through your work and service.

Though I suggest patience with the evolutionary process, be sure to continually refine your ideal client dossier so you know who to take on and who to decline as your business continues to grow. You'll likely add multiple ideal client profiles to your business *verticals*. For example, if you begin to do new construction design, you may want to list the types of builders you want to work with, so be sure to create a profile for builders.

There will be times when your pipeline of projects is slow and you'll be tempted to take on clients who you know in your gut are not right for you. Financial fear will take over from time to time, but that doesn't mean you should take on non-ideal clients, as they can cost you more in the long run.

In 2010, Kathy, one of my earliest coaching clients, fought me on defining her ideal client profile. But I pushed her to create it and, before long, she was earning a multi-six-figure income, which was the same as her revenue the year she started coaching with me.

A few years later, Kathy had her first VIP Day during October High Point Market. I'll never forget our conversation about affluent clients—she said that she wanted to work with them because they had large or unlimited budgets. While she did work with them on occasion at that time, she found herself struggling because she didn't like some of her clients, who were bullies.

Kathy made money from these high-end projects, but the price was high: she was stressed and often lost sleep. I remember her bursting into tears when I told her she should consider not taking clients just because they could afford her. I added that it was more important that she focus on her personal values and work only with people who had similar beliefs. She deserved to be respected for her talent, and I advised her to say no to those difficult clients.

Creating a Marketing Plan

You should have a written marketing plan that you schedule and execute in ninety-day sprints. Never forget that your job as a business owner is to be the rainmaker; you're responsible for bringing in money to pay your team and ensure that you reach your desired financial results.

The purpose of great marketing is to make selling irrelevant. Remember, as you build a plan, the easiest way to get more referrals is to wow your clients with a great experience, which should be non-salesy. Also, whatever you do, be patient—it can take up to fourteen connections with your brand for prospects to reach out when they are in the market to hire someone with your skills.

If your pipeline is empty, start with reaching out to past clients with handwritten notes, letting them know that you're thinking about them and that you hope they're still enjoying their home. You can also remind them that you grow your business by referrals, and if they know of anyone who would benefit from your services, you'd greatly appreciate the connection.

Many of your clients may also be business owners, so they will understand that giving you a referral would be the kind and helpful thing to do. Once you ask a few times and get positive results, you'll find that it gets easier to ask. We're all in the business of relationships, and if your clients appreciate you, they'll be happy to help.

Reaping the Rewards of Powerful Marketing

Now that you know what you need to do to build your business in the early stages, let's return to Barbara's story. She worked tirelessly at marketing and, within months, she was invited into our Charter Boardroom because her business exceeded the one-million-dollar mark. Even as a business owner who was in her early thirties, she quickly earned the respect of the other Boardroom members for her business acumen and drive. She built her Instagram following to well over 200,000 followers as of this book's publication date and, a few years later, she rebranded her businesses to fit her future vision.

Today, she is successfully running an online business named after her adorable kids. She has built three distinct businesses. Barbara has clarity about her vision, who her ideal clients are, and what her brand message is, and she has visuals to match her design style. When you see her work, you get a sense of the person behind the brand. As a result of this, Barbara has grown her business nearly six times in five years.

This is possible for you as well. It takes clear vision, a plan to build your business, and determination to succeed. If you're passionate about what you do, you'll find a way to create an amazing business that generates a great income.

Summary

- Create your ideal client dossier and don't deviate from it for your financial and emotional sanity. It's not worth the money to suffer from difficult clients. Make sure your clients are aligned with your values.

- Create a simple marketing plan in the early stages of your business to achieve your goals.

- Focus on relationship building.

- Market every day without fail.

- Your brand is more than your graphic logo and collaterals; it includes your values and culture. It includes every client experience and every touchpoint with your clients. It is who you are, how you dress and present yourself, and it is your company's client service. It's everything!

- Measure your Return on Investment (ROI) for each marketing dollar spent. You should earn back more than the dollars you spend.

- Your brand visuals should be consistent with your design style. Working with a branding company that understands your industry is important and should be done when you're in Phase 2 of your business, Rapid Growth (i.e., $250K to $999K).

- If you need help with learning how to market yourself, consider attending our 5-Day Marketing Blueprint Challenge, which we hold twice a year.

CHAPTER 11

Simple Marketing and Mindset Shifts to Create Fast Results

Your destiny is determined by your decisions.

—TONY ROBBINS

Now that you've read this far, it is time to ask yourself again what you really want for your life and business. We talked earlier about having a ten-year vision, but since it was so early in the process of thinking about your long-term goals, let's revisit your vision one more time.

We've spent time going through many critical factors that you must employ to run a successful business. I'm guessing and hoping you're more determined than ever to run your own design company, or perhaps you now believe it will require too much work and I've helped you decide to find another profession. (This has happened with clients in the past.) Either way is fine—if your ultimate goal is to love your life, and your work takes up the majority of your waking hours, then we want you to love all aspects of your career.

A Strategy for Success

In *The Art of War*, Chinese military strategist Sun Tzu said, "Tactics without strategy is the noise before defeat." But what is strategy?

According to *Forbes*, "Strategy is a framework for making decisions about how you will play the game of business." It is a way of planning so you see the vision or end goal ahead and, by working backward, you decide what steps or tactics will be used to achieve your goals.

Strategy is especially effective when you accept that you're really the CEO of a business that happens to provide design services. For many designers, the thought of being a CEO may feel odd. In fact, a client told us she was getting ready to print new business cards and wanted to know from other Boardroom members in our Slack channel what title she should use. I suggested "CEO and Principal Designer." She was clearly uncomfortable with the CEO title; it felt more natural to her to be the principal designer. I have had the same conversation with other successful design firm owners, who also feel uncomfortable with that moniker. It is clear that being a business owner is not how many designers or creative entrepreneurs self-identify.

If you don't feel comfortable with being a CEO, why is that? The CEO is responsible for managing the company and making decisions, and that is what you do every day. If it feels awkward to think of yourself as a CEO, you might want to spend some time journaling to figure out why. As you become more confident as a businessperson, you may grow into the title. If you are dealing with high-level, C-suite executives, do you think they might identify you as a professional business executive who happens to do design?

Confidence Is Key

Courage and confidence are learnable skills. As you face seemingly insurmountable odds, know that your power is on the other side of fear.

A CEO must be courageous and willing to do things that other people wouldn't choose to do, even if it is uncomfortable, unsettling, and unnerving. Building courage develops with practice. Stepping fearlessly into hard situations and making choices even (and especially) when it is uncomfortable is true courage. If you were protecting your child, you would do whatever it took, even if it was uncomfortable. Your business is also your baby.

Look at every challenging situation as an opportunity to learn how strong and powerful you are. By stepping into the ring, you'll soon find yourself solving problems effectively and feeling more confident.

Learn to Be Decisive

Some people find decisiveness easy, but some endlessly rethink and overthink their decisions. That indecisiveness doesn't necessarily lead to a better decision. If you're struggling with making decisions, these may be contributing factors:

- **Fear of making a mistake because it might be wrong** You can always make a different decision, learn from it, and move on. Few decisions are life-altering, so save yourself the mental anguish and discomfort.

- **Fear of losing money** By making a decision, could you lose all of your money or just a small portion? If it is under a certain amount, it makes more sense to move forward, as long as you won't be put in a dire circumstance due to the expenditure. If the decision results in an ROI that is many times the initial cost, then it makes more sense to move forward because it truly is a no-risk situation.

- **Fear of comparison** You may fear that someone important to you would do something differently. Does that really matter, or is it more important to decide on your criteria for making a good decision? Will it improve your life? Will it improve your business? Will it save you valuable time? Will it result in more profit? Will it relieve you of something you don't enjoy? Comparison is irrelevant when you consider these questions.

- **Low self-esteem** Maybe you don't feel worthy, so it is hard to make a decision that would be in your best interest because you don't feel that you should have the result you're considering working toward. But what if you made the decision anyway? Your self-worth will grow as a result of making great decisions, and that comes with practice.

- **Too many options** Studies have shown that having more than three options makes it very hard for people to decide what to do. Try trimming your list first, then prioritize and set a date on which you'll make the decision.

- **Emotional reasons** Often, we struggle with a decision because we are emotionally connected to a person, a memory, or a possession. Emotional pain is real and hard to manage. If you can focus on the logical reasons to make a decision, it will be easier to move forward. To remove the emotion from your decision, try writing down a complete statement of the problem, list the options, put a stake in the ground, and go with what appears to be the best decision. You'll spend much less time in emotional distress.

The benefits of quick decision-making far outweigh the possible effects of a decision that isn't optimal. You'll save time and energy and, more importantly, you'll gain respect for yourself and the respect of others, especially those who also struggle with making decisions.

Not making a decision is also a decision—it's death by a thousand cuts. The faster you make a decision and move on, the better off you'll be. Even if the decision you make isn't the best one you could have made, at least you can adjust from the new position and you'll quit worrying if what you did was right or wrong. You don't want someone else to make a decision for you.

Set a time and number limit on decisions each day to avoid fatigue. For example, the president doesn't make small decisions, such as what to wear or eat, because he (or, hopefully in the future, she) has bigger, more important commitments.

Limiting decisions will also help with your design process. Rethinking and reselecting can result in many lost hours on projects. If you're indecisive, your client will have less confidence and trust in you. Learn to make decisions and stick with them. For example, instead of taking five hours to look for the perfect accessory (that you can't bill for), set a time limit of one hour to find a *good enough* choice.

Your confidence will grow immeasurably if you apply decisiveness, since you won't be waffling and worrying. What's better than knowing that you've done your very best to make a great decision?

Decisions also factor into what you'll take away from this book. Prioritize your list and add the goals you want to achieve in your calendar, just as you would a personal appointment with your doctor or a client.

Giving Goals Focus

We can lose countless hours of each day on tasks that don't move us toward our destination. You've probably read that multitasking is inefficient; this is especially true when you're working on creative design tasks (right brain) and pivot to accounting or budgeting (left brain). Try to do all your creative tasks in a row, then move on to everything else. Your brain will be able to function more efficiently.

With technology, it is easy to get distracted and go down rabbit holes. You can't charge for time in rabbit holes, and we all know that time is money. When you need to do detailed or focused work like drawings, planning, and so on, turn off all distractions. Put your phone away. Turn off any messaging apps. Find an app to help you better manage your time, such as Focus Timer. There are several out there that can block you from visiting distracting sites and track how much time you spend on activities. A timer can be extremely helpful to make you more aware of your bad habits so you can learn better skills.

Focus timers can also be set for *pomodoros*—specific chunks of time that are allocated for a particular activity. For example, you can set a twenty-five-minute timer to select finishes for a bathroom. Once the timer goes off, take five minutes to do something unrelated to work—drink a glass of water, walk around the block, pet your cat, or get a snack. Pomodoros are great for getting big projects done efficiently. For example, I've been writing for three hours with study music in the background. I allow myself five-minute breaks to check Slack (our communication software) or get up and stretch.

Keep in mind that focus can be made more difficult with the temptation to answer the phone, reply to a text message, or answer "do you have a minute?" questions. Though people on your team may need answers, try to block out periods in which you're not distracted. Some owners suggest that their employees wear headphones to stay focused, and I agree. A quiet workplace is a more efficient work environment.

Personal Management

This is one of the skills that most of us struggle to conquer. I have momentary lapses, even though I know what works best for me. Here a few suggestions:

- **Morning rituals** You may be aware that the most successful people have rituals they follow to ensure they have a great start to their day. They get up at the same time every day and do specific things to get their brains focused and engaged. For example, if you set your alarm to go off at the same time every day and, when you wake up, drink a glass of water, followed by meditation or prayer, you'll be mentally prepared for the rest of the day. You might then exercise for an hour, eat breakfast, take a shower, and then spend some time journaling or reading.

- **The next chunk of time, if used for projects, can get you ahead for the day** Use your focus timer or your cell phone to train your brain to work in small chunks of time. If you can get two hours of work done on a project or on moving your business forward, you'll be productive and efficient.

- **Plan your days around similar activities** For example, I often suggest that business owners do most of their billable work on Tuesdays, Wednesdays, and Thursdays. If they block seven hours per day for billable work on those days, they'll meet their 50 percent of billable hours easily.

- **Schedule other meetings and project work time around your billable time** If this tip is the only one you apply from this book, it can change your life and your bank account dramatically. For example, if you bill twenty hours per week out of fifty weeks a year (assuming you take two weeks off), that's 1,000 hours. If your hourly rate is $150, you should be able to bill $150,000 per year just in design fees. How much would that impact your life? Be sure to review your P&L statement to see where you are today to set a goal for the next twelve months.

- **Plan time to mentor and train employees and have team meetings** The more training and mentoring you provide, the more likely you are to have employees who are also efficiently providing design services to your clients. Two to four hours per week is advised. Marketing requires a minimum of ten hours per week, which can also be delegated or outsourced.

- **Plan time to think; it a highly undervalued skill** I mentioned this to one of my clients who asked, "What am I supposed to be thinking about?" My response was "Planning, visioning, goal setting, problem-solving, etc." We all need quiet, uninterrupted time to think. If you don't have this time already mapped out on your calendar, then add at least two hours per week.

If you can implement these suggestions, you'll find that your time is more efficient, you're less overwhelmed, and you'll be able to knock out a lot of work quickly. You will even have more time to see friends and family, vacation, and engage in other fun activities.

While we're on the subject of fun, I strongly recommend that you schedule time for rest and relaxation. I start my annual planning with scheduling my vacations first. As a matter of fact, I've already scheduled my first five-week sabbatical at the end of the year. The team knows and, with it already on my calendar, I will start preparing for being away for that length of time. I'll ensure that the team has everything they need from me and that I've completed projects.

Similarly, if you're planning to have a baby, then you'll also want to have a plan to prepare your team (or hire someone to help) during maternity leave. One of my clients, Catherine, decided to take four months off and transitioned management of her team to her design director. When she got back from maternity leave, she felt like a guest in her business because the team had a new reporting structure. She also suggested adding business development to the plan. She was doing most of the sales prior to her leave and, while she was off, no one was tasked with marketing.

Resilience, Determination, and Consistency

Running a business requires the ability to bounce back when things aren't going well. When the 2008 recession hit, we struggled for a few years, and what we learned was invaluable. We found it satisfying when we reflected on how we overcame the challenges. I'm sure you will as well as you manage your response to the economy, the election, the pandemic, or other personal concerns. You will quickly develop processes to bounce back. Your resilience can be increased by coming up with strategies before the unexpected occurs. For example: If XYZ happens, I'll do ABC.

As you read earlier, my husband tried to talk me into finding another job several times. I wasn't willing to quit, and now he is happy I didn't. As he said to me, "There's a reason I'm not running a business!" He tried to run a computer shop with friends years ago and realized he wasn't cut out for the stress, risk, and responsibility required.

If you're reading this book, then, of course, you have a certain amount of determination to succeed. You can also amp it up by reviewing your goals every day and journaling about them. Even one email to a key contact will make a difference.

Whatever you do consistently will show up later in your life and in your checkbook, so be sure you're working on things that will move your business and life forward. If you're not satisfied with the results, then you need to examine the activities you're doing to figure out what needs to change. One great tool to use is Toyota's "Five Whys": Keep asking why at least five times until you uncover the root cause of your problem. For example:

- Why do I attract difficult clients?

- Why is the problem repeating itself?

- Why can't I acknowledge something that I should be doing to prevent this (such as not sticking to the ideal client dossier)?

- Why am I not sticking to the ideal client dossier (i.e., fear of cash flow)?

- If it is a fear of cash flow, then why am I not marketing more consistently to get great leads?

Now that you understand this process, pull this method out of your toolkit when you're struggling. You want to fix the underlying problem and not the superficial situation you're experiencing—this strategy will serve you well in business and in life.

Organizational psychologist and author Dr. Benjamin Hardy says, "Going through the motions is not enough. There isn't a checklist of things you must do to be successful. You have to fundamentally change who you are to live at a higher level. You must go from doing to being—so that what you do is a reflection of who you are, and who you're becoming. Once you've experienced this change, success will be natural" (2017, "34

Things You Need to Give Up to Be Successful"). In the early stages of your business, you'll feel frustration, fear, and terror but also sparkling moments of joy. You get to create your vision and something that changes your life and the lives of your family, friends, and community.

Being honest about your current skill gaps and seeking to fill them will change your business. You will become more assured and committed as you see its evolution with small changes implemented consistently. You don't want to repeat the same mistakes five, ten, or twenty years from now; you want to achieve new heights. And you deserve it!

Summary

If I were to pick one area for you to focus on after figuring out your long-term vision and goals, it would be the mindset around marketing. Here are some tips to make your marketing strategy successful.

- If you don't like the money that's in your checkbook, then get busy with marketing. Daily. Consistently. Learn to love it.

- Ask for referrals regularly.

- Build the referral request process into your onboarding process with your clients. Let them know that you grow your business by referrals. When they're happy, remind them that you would love a referral.

- Measure your results and track your leads.

- Work on your mindset, including making faster and better decisions, managing your time, and solving your problems quickly.

- Having a marketing mindset is one of the keys to running a successful and profitable business.

Conclusion

Thank you for taking the time to read this book. My goal was to help you identify and overcome your skills, gaps, and mindset roadblocks. Maybe your results won't change from just one reading, but over time, you'll expand your capabilities and believe in yourself as the leader, entrepreneur, and amazing designer or creative entrepreneur that I know you are.

I hope you're energized and excited about your future as the CEO of your interior design business. You deserve to be successful and well compensated for your contribution to your client's well-being, happiness, and function in the beautiful homes you've created.

In Chapter 1, we talked about financial knowledge and how you are not alone with feeling overwhelmed by numbers. So many of my clients have felt intimidated with understanding this new language, but once they learn it, they are happy and confident and never have to worry about that lack of knowledge again. This quote from Jim Rohn exemplifies how I feel about learning: "Don't wish it was easier; wish you were better. Don't wish for less problems; wish for more skills" (https://www.jimrohn.com/10-unforgettable-quotes-by-jim-rohn/).

In Chapter 2, we discussed how important your vision is for future success. Without a compelling vision, we coast through life getting by but not achieving all that we're meant to accomplish. I have a bigger vision for you than you may have at this moment, and I see the potential in my clients. I see what stops them cold and prevents them from enjoying the creation of something that could never be done without their unique point of view and personality. I want you to believe that you're capable of far more than you realize. You're a unicorn—in a good way.

We also talked about negative or fixed mindset. It's important to identify what's in your way. A particular thought pattern holds you back from incredible success. Just knowing what it is that triggers you to think negatively will help you eliminate that block. Focusing on what you do right is more valuable than negative self-talk, which destroys your motivation and belief in yourself.

In Chapter 3, we discussed the concept of building your business from the inside out by thinking about what you want and why, your values, and the culture you want to create. Think about your point of view—how does it relate to your design aesthetic? Do you believe that families with small kids and pets can enjoy clean, white rooms? Do you believe that quality can't be compromised when making design decisions? Do you think that comfort is physical or also visual? How did you come to that conclusion? Write your story about your point of view and how you came to it because it is important that your clients know who you are and why they should care about working with you.

It's important to be authentically rooted in who you are. No one else can be you—your story is different. I remember after we started our business many years ago, I went to another consultant's website, and I was shocked to read my story on her site as if it were hers. Needless to say, within months, her website was gone, and I never heard about her again. So, remember, be your best you.

Chapter 4 focused on systems and processes you need in your business. Anything that is done more than once needs a documented system, process, or checklist. Even though most of us love the creative aspect of what we do, if we want to scale our businesses to generate more money and freedom, we must have duplicatable systems that others can execute in the same way we do.

Our brand, whether we realize it or not, includes everything that we do. How do your employees answer the phone? How do you onboard clients or resolve problems? These questions are important for you to consider. If you want to be able to take long vacations, make sure that the wheels won't fall off the bus while you're gone. Plan to make the business independent of your time and effort. Make it dependent on your well-designed ecosystem of people, processes, and systems.

We talked about building a team in Chapter 5. Designers often struggle with hiring because they don't know when and who to hire, how much to pay, and how to manage, mentor, or lead employees.

You're not born with management or leadership skills, though you may show some great talent for getting people to do what you want them to do. I failed miserably in my first business, and I think my employees would agree. Though we grew rapidly and got amazing jobs, I made the mistake of micromanaging due to fear. It was scary to run the business and be responsible for so many people's livelihoods. Mistakes were expensive and came out of my pocket. I hired good people, and it was important to let them do their job without me looking over their shoulders. Some flourished in spite of me.

It's important to give people the opportunity to make their own mistakes because that's how we learn. Ask your employees how they think a problem can be solved and how they can avoid the same situation in the future. Don't beat them up; they didn't intentionally make the mistake. I hope you'll learn from my errors and set boundaries, delegate outcomes, and manage expectations.

Consider your contribution to the problem. Did you give employees good guidance and training? Did you document your systems and processes to avoid those problems? If not, start and accept your part in the failure. It's okay—it really is just money.

Chapter 6 shared management and leadership tips and, yes, they are different. Mentoring is another aspect of running your business. If you start there and know that your job is to remove roadblocks from your employees, provide clear direction, and set expectations, you'll have an easier time running your business.

Delegating is different than abdicating. I still catch myself abdicating from time to time, so just be aware of your tendency to assign tasks without ensuring the other person has all of the tools, skills, and information to finish the job to your level of expectation.

Chapter 7 focused on how to charge for your services and products. Many of the concepts may be familiar, but you must still decide what the best way is for you to operate your business profitably. I provided you with options and some special wording to express the value of the items that you charge for so that your clients don't think of your fees as just costs. You want them to understand the value of each type of service or product that you sell.

Selling is essential to your business success. That sentence may make you feel queasy, but you sell yourself to get clients, then you sell your ideas, and you may spend a good bit of time selling your clients on paying your bills. Work on your confidence about the value you provide. Be willing to hear the client's point of view, but also be firm when explaining how and why you charge a certain way. They rarely understand how long things take, which can lead to unhappy clients who decide to terminate the contract.

Set expectations and keep in mind that you may have to repeat the message as many as seven times for the client to understand how you charge and what is reasonable. Even if you work with clients who *don't have budgets*, they still need to have a comfort level with what they're willing to invest. If you can't talk openly about the fees before you get started, it is guaranteed that you'll run into issues during the process of the engagement. The more confident you are with what you charge, the more clients will relax and trust you. Talk frequently about where you are so they aren't surprised. Sticker shock can cause tremendous stress for you and the client, so avoid it by being proactive with your communication.

Chapter 8 focused on financials, which you should review until you truly understand them because they are essential to your success as a business owner. We discussed three main financial statements and how to understand them at the highest level. Over time, reading them will be second nature.

Especially when business feels chaotic, it's imperative to have a cash flow statement to anticipate future bills and cash out. Without understanding and forecasting your cash flow, you'll be in a constant state of stress trying to bring in clients and do business. It's a juggling act for all owners, unless they've systematized their business to generate leads.

Chapter 9 was about planning for profit. I've never had a coaching client come to me with a profit plan; they tell me what they want to earn, which is typically in the multiple six figures, but they have no idea how to get there. Review this chapter to discover how to plan. It's not as hard as you might think. You can make multiple six figures as an interior designer, and if you think that would make your life better, then set at least six figures as your income goal for next year. The only one stopping you from achieving your dreams and desired income is you.

Chapter 10 focused on the simple ways you can market your business in two phases. Many designers think they need to focus all of their efforts on social media, almost to the detriment of building a strong marketing foundation. You need a beautiful website, and social media is best focused on Phase 2 of your business, after you've established relationships and referrals.

Building relationships during all phases of your business is important. Usually, if your business is not where it needs to be, you don't have enough of the right relationships. Always think about who you need to meet with and plan connection time into your schedule. It's actually fun and, remember, relationships are everything!

Finally, in Chapter 11, I shared the key skills and mindset traits that will help you become a stronger business owner. Ninety percent of what you do every day is run a business that happens to provide design services.

Plan on improving one skill per month. The first one you should focus on is the one that is causing you the biggest problems or holding you back from your biggest and most audacious goals.

Summary

As your business grows past Phase 1, Business Breakthrough ($0 to $249K), you should only be thinking about strategy and doing less of the day-to-day tasks in your business. During Phase 2, Rapid Growth, business development should become your primary focus. You are the networker and connector, and your marketing team is responsible for the everyday work of serving your ideal clients. In the next book, *Rapid Growth*, we'll talk more about marketing at this level of your business. The goal is to have such a great marketing system in place that it makes *selling* irrelevant.

There are three key success accelerators for your business:

- **Business model** You need a financial, foundational, and operational model that takes you from where you are now to where you want to go. It requires thinking deeply about the profit and income you want to earn more than the top-line revenue number that most people focus on achieving. You need to know how to charge and get paid for the value you provide. We call this the Creative Value Blueprint™.

- **Belief breakthrough** You need the right mindset around prosperity, purpose, and power so you can confidently navigate the waters of running your business.

- **Community** We all need information, support, and encouragement, and that's what we love about our clients: They share their challenges and successes, and they love each other. It's an amazing community of like-minded peers who enjoy the business of design and want to grow with you and see you succeed. Our community also includes a great coaching team and other experts who support our clients' businesses with their specific expertise.

You can accomplish whatever you dream of, and I know you'll do it faster than you ever expected if you take to heart what you learned in this book. Be sure to share your big wins with me. If you have questions and you'd like to find out how we can help you, I'd love to hear from you!

Resources

We can't wait to meet you at an industry event or at one of our own events. We have many shortcuts and programs to help you navigate the choppy waters of growing your business successfully.

We encourage you to visit the Creative Value Blueprint™ Resource Page for one or all of the following resources:

- Your Current Reality Assessment, including a short video from me about your results

- Profit & Pricing Shortcuts, which include:
  - Easy Budget Calculator and training video
  - Ideal Client Dossier
  - 10 Biggest Mistakes Designers Make with Fees
  - How to Hire a Coach or Consultant

- Join our Leadership Collective, which includes:
  - Circle
  - Alliance
  - Boardroom

- Upcoming Challenges, which include:
  - 5-Day Financial Blueprint Challenge
  - 5-Day Marketing Blueprint Challenge
  - Planning Challenge
- Virtual 2-Day Genius Exchange
- Creative Genius Podcast

About Gail Doby

Gail Doby is co-founder of Gail Doby Coaching & Consulting, a firm that helps designers, architects, and other creatives increase profitability by up to 512 percent. As the firm's Chief Visionary Officer, Doby does more than help clients wrangle decimals on a budget sheet. After running her own Denver-based design firm (plus a BSBA in Finance and Banking), she's obsessed with sharing innovative ways to overcome business roadblocks, challenges, and detours creative entrepreneurs face when doing it on their own. (She also works as a strategist, brand builder, marketer, operations manager, human resource advisor, and sometimes therapist.) No matter which hat she is wearing, her goal is simple—to empower design-industry clients to differentiate themselves, drive measurable results, achieve business projections, and create personal satisfaction through game-changing strategies and business practices.

Her ultimate achievement? Helping hardworking designers work smart. "Running a business can feel lonely and full of challenges," explains Doby. "Many designers are great at design, but have little business training, and working for others can, in some cases, be a lesson in what not to do."

"Some designers we know fell into running a business," she continues. "They became unexpected entrepreneurs as they moved from working for others to working for themselves. Suddenly they were deep into the design work but completely unprepared to run a company. Really talented designers falter—not for lack of design talent or intelligence—but because they do not have the tools, guidance, or support to create a healthy business."

Gail's Ten Favorite Books for Emerging Entrepreneurs

1. *The Miracle Morning: The Not-So-Obvious Secret Guaranteed to Transform Your Life (Before 8 AM)*, Hal Elrod

2. *Personality Isn't Permanent: Break Free from Self-Limiting Beliefs and Rewrite Your Story*, Benjamin Hardy, PhD

3. *The Code of the Extraordinary Mind: 10 Unconventional Laws to Redefine Your Life and Succeed on Your Own Terms*, Vishen Lakhiani

4. *Letting Go: The Pathway of Surrender*, David R. Hawkins, MD, PhD

5. *Eat That Frog!: 21 Great Ways to Stop Procrastinating and Get More Done in Less Time*, Brian Tracy

6. *Atomic Habits: An Easy & Proven Way to Build Good Habits & Break Bad Ones*, James Clear

7. *The Toilet Paper Entrepreneur: The Tell-It-Like-It-Is Guide to Cleaning Up in Business, Even if You Are at the End of Your Roll*, Mike Michalowicz

8. *The Pumpkin Plan: A Simple Strategy to Grow a Remarkable Business in Any Field*, Mike Michalowicz

9. *The Go-Giver: A Little Story About a Powerful Business Idea*, Bob Burg

10. *Endless Referrals: Network Your Everyday Contacts into Sales*, Bob Burg

Financial Glossary

Word	Definition
Assets	Assets are what you own, including cash, savings, works in progress, accounts receivable, vendor deposits, inventory, building(s), automobile(s), equipment, furniture, etc.
Balance sheet	A financial statement that shows your assets (cash, accounts receivable, inventory, works in progress, owned buildings or assets), liabilities (what you owe for loans, credit cards, sales tax, etc.), and owner's equity. A balance sheet shows your financial position since you started your business.
Burdened costs	All expenses related to having employees on your team. Burdened costs include taxes, insurance, cell phones, gifts, 401(k) contributions by your company, training, etc. When you include your income, add in things such as car operating expenses.
Cash flow forecast	A prediction of when cash will be received from revenue and when it will be paid out for expenses, like rent or cost of goods sold.
Cost of goods sold (COGS)	The direct costs and purchases incurred by your business for client projects. Put another way, COGS is money spent that generates sales. This includes furniture, frames, fabric, trim, subcontractor fees (i.e., CAD work, etc.) and their burdened costs, freight costs associated with client projects, etc.
Equity	What your company is worth after subtracting all liabilities from all assets. It is a cumulative total for all of the years you've been in business.

Gross profit	Gross profit = revenue - cost of goods sold. Gross profit is expressed in dollars.
Gross profit margin	Gross profit margin = gross profit ÷ total revenue. Gross profit margin is expressed as a percentage.
Income statement/ profit & loss statement	Also known as a P&L, this statement includes your total revenue, cost of goods sold, operating costs, and net profit. It is a snapshot of your company's current year performance. It can be either a monthly, year-to-date, or annual statement.
Liabilities	What you owe. This includes credit card balance(s), outstanding loans, mortgage(s), sales tax payable, taxes payable, etc.
Net profit	Net profit = total revenue - cost of goods sold - operating expenses. The total amount left over after paying all expenses.
Net profit margin	Net profit margin = net profit ÷ total revenue. A margin is expressed as a percentage.
Overhead	All expenses to operate your business, whether you make sales or not. Examples of operating expenses include rent, utilities, insurance, marketing expenses, administrative salaries and burdened costs, meals, professional services, travel, etc.
Revenue	All sales generated by your business. This includes design fees and product sales, like furniture and draperies.